THE WITNESS HOUSE

THE
WITNESS
HOUSE

Nazis and Holocaust Survivors
Sharing a Villa During
the Nuremberg Trials

CHRISTIANE KOHL

Translated by Anthea Bell

OTHER PRESS
New York

Production Editor: *Yvonne E. Cárdenas*
Text Designer: *Simon M. Sullivan*
This book was set in 10.25 pt Sabon by Alpha Design &
Composition of Pittsfield, NH.

10 9 8 7 6 5 4 3 2 1

Library of Congress Cataloging-in-Publication Data

Kohl, Christiane, 1954–
[Zeugenhaus. English]
The witness house : nazis and holocaust survivors sharing a villa
during the nuremberg trials / By Christiane Kohl ; Translated by
Anthea Bell.
p. cm.
Includes bibliographical references and index.
ISBN 978-1-59051-379-8 (pbk. original with flaps) —
ISBN 978-1-59051-380-4 (e-book) 1. Nuremberg Trial of Major
German War Criminals, Nuremberg, Germany, 1945–1946.
2. Nuremberg War Crime Trials, Nuremberg, Germany,
1946–1949. 3. Kálnoky, Ingeborg. 4. Witnesses—Germany—
Nuremberg—Biography. 5. Boardinghouses—Germany—
Nuremberg—History—20th century. I. Title.
KZ1176.5.K6613 2010
341.6'90268—dc22
2010011435

CONTENTS

THE WITNESS HOUSE

TWO VISITORS' BOOKS
AND A SUSPICION

If my friend Wolfgang hadn't been there, the two old gentlemen would probably never have turned to the subject. As it was, however, they suddenly began telling stories in competition with each other. We were sitting by the big window in the living room of my parents' house, an old water mill that had been converted into a handsome dwelling years before. By day there was a wonderful view of the green countryside from that window, but now it was dark, and only the pale glow of our table lamp lit up the trees on the banks of the nearby stream. Their shapes loomed like sinister figures in the dark night. My father had brought up a good bottle of wine from the cellar, and we were a cheerful party. Then the conversation touched upon the delicate subject of the past.

My father had talked to me about the war before; he had been shot down three times flying a dive-bomber, and ended up as a POW. But it was a different kind of story that he told us now. He seemed to find it an awkward subject, although he laughed again and again as he told us about those difficult days in 1930s Berlin when he was studying law in the city. The Nazi period had coincided with his youth, and I had always felt sure that he could not have lived through such turmoil entirely unaffected. But whenever I asked more about it, he would give me only a vague answer.

That evening, however, was different. My father spoke in detail, and more frankly than ever before, about his experiences of daily life under National Socialism. That prompted our long-term houseguest, Bernhard, to respond with a number of anecdotes of his own. At this time Bernhard von Kleist was seventy-nine years old, with pale blue eyes and a slight limp as the result of a war wound, and he had been living for several years at the Bear Mill, my parents' house in North Hesse. He was good at entertaining my mother, who all her life feared nothing so much as boredom.

There was often a good deal of petty sniping between Bernhard and my father, but at the moment all was peace and harmony. They both talked freely, and only the crackling of the fire on the hearth sometimes rose above the flow of their reminiscences. My mother pointedly turned to watch the flames. She hated it when the conversation in our house turned to serious subjects. My friend Wolfgang Korruhn, well-known as a television journalist, was planning to make a documentary about the involvement of the IG Farben chemical company in the systematic murder of the Jews by the Nazis. Bernhard von Kleist was interesting on that subject, for he had been an interpreter at the Nuremberg trials. We sat talking for a long time. Later that night I made some notes, so I can still remember almost every detail of our discussion. It was the evening of August 31, 1980.

Bernhard left us for a moment, went to his own room, and soon came back with a rather worn-looking album under his arm. It was bound in pale brown leather with a thin, rectangular gold line adorning the cover, and the pages too were edged with a very thin layer of gold leaf. Carefully, as if it were a treasure box, the old gentleman opened the book. The pages that came into view were yellowing slightly, and were inscribed in a wide variety of different hands—this little leather-bound volume was a visitors' book. Bernhard von Kleist carefully leafed through it, and quickly found several entries where men who worked for IG Farben had left their mark for posterity in the form of sententious truisms. A manager in the chemical company made grateful mention, in elaborate handwriting adorned with flourishes, of "the sweetening of bitter hours." Bernhard von Kleist vaguely remembered that this man had been summoned to give evidence in the Nuremberg courthouse on the development of Zyklon B, the pesticide used to kill millions of people in the death camps.

There were many names in the visitors' book. Some were in ornately flowing handwriting that was difficult to decipher. I could make out others almost at first glance. Robert Havemann, a member of the Resistance to the Nazi regime and later a dissident in East Germany, had entered his name. A few pages further on I saw the signature of Fritz Wiedemann—"Former adjutant to Adolf Hitler," Bernhard explained in response to my questioning glance. "He became a good friend to us," he added almost proudly. The journalist Eugen Kogon, a long-term inmate of the Buchenwald concentration camp, appeared in the visitors' book, and so did a man called Edinger Ancker, who according to his entry had worked for the notorious Nazi leader Martin Bormann. I saw the dashing signature of Rudolf Diels—"Founder of the Gestapo," Kleist made haste to explain. And I read the name of one Gisa Punzengruber scrawled in the book. Underneath it, someone had added in pencil "Concentration camp witness."

As I leafed on and on through the book, I began to feel a shiver run down my spine. How could all these very different people have left their names in one and the same visitors' book, so soon after the end of the Nazi period? What had brought them together, and why?

The answer was that the visitors' book came from a "witness house" where people stayed when they were to give evidence at the Nuremberg war crimes trials. The witnesses stayed in two adjoining villas on the outskirts of Nuremberg, said Kleist. His wife, Annemarie, who had been dead for many years now, was the manager of the two houses for a time. The atmosphere there must have been nothing short of extraordinary, for as the entries in the visitors' book showed, Nazi functionaries and former Resistance members had stayed there under the same roof at the same time. While it was easy enough for victims of the Nazis to avoid their persecutors elsewhere, in the fall of 1945 they sat together around a table almost every evening in this house.

"What on earth was it like?" Wolfgang and I exclaimed almost in unison. We wanted to know every last detail of this remarkable guesthouse. But Kleist was visibly evasive about answering that question. "Oh, they played a lot of bridge," said the old man slowly, drawing on his cigarette. "They smoked cigars, drank American whisky, discussed the problems of the time. I hardly need to say," he added in a pedantic tone, "that the guests generally behaved like gentlemen even when the situation was difficult."

As far as I remember, Wolfgang never made his film about IG Farben, but that evening started me on research that was to occupy my mind for many years. What exactly had happened in that house just after the war, when recent German history had been so close to the surface? The yellowing pages of Bernhard's visitors' book were evidence of something not to be found in any court records: the fears and delusions of those who had been followers of the Nazi regime, as well as the bitterness and anger of its surviving victims. The guests in the Witness House—this was my initial thought—had firsthand knowledge of issues that still concern Germans today: Nazi crimes, accusations of guilt, denials of personal responsibility. Again and again they must have wondered how those incredible crimes could ever have been committed.

One of the men who had known the house well was Robert M. W. Kempner. The former U.S. prosecutor stayed on in Germany after the end of the Nuremberg trials, and set up a law practice in Frankfurt. A few years after that evening in the old mill, I met him at a hotel in Königstein where he often stayed at this time. The Hotel Sonnenhof was a handsome villa with little turrets and bay windows, set in extensive grounds, and had a wonderful view of the landscape.

Inside, the hotel had a certain rather faded charm; the upholstered chairs were well-worn and the chair covers threadbare. Kempner was sitting in the Green Salon, a room with large windows looking out on the grounds. Beside him sat his assistant of many years, Jane Lester; I was to see a good deal of her later. The pair were not the sort of people you meet every day: Kempner, then in his late eighties, had snow-white hair and deeply hooded eyes, but he sat very upright, and still seemed the forceful figure he had been during the Nuremberg trials. Jane Lester, a delicately built woman with long, graying hair, who had worked for Kempner ever since Nuremberg, must have been very attractive in her youth. She now appeared reserved, but it was easy to see that of the two she was really the one who held the reins.

Kempner still had vivid memories of the house and its guests. He had already written, in his memoirs, that it had been "no mean achievement" to accommodate witnesses of wholly different political leanings in the same place "and do it with sensitivity." Now he told me that tensions sometimes ran high. Some of the guests had been notorious for their relationships with women, and that, said the old gentleman, smiling, led to all kinds of complications both in and outside the house. When Kempner, who was rather deaf, failed to catch a question of mine, Jane Lester repeated it to him. She herself had now lived in Germany for many decades, but she retained a strong American accent, and her voice still sounded as if she had only just arrived from the United States.

After a while Kempner mentioned the lady who managed the Witness House: "A Hungarian countess, blonde, blue-eyed, and pretty as a picture," he said, hinting that she herself had been one of the ladies so much sought after at the time of the Nuremberg trials. "There were a great many unattached men, and a number of attractive women," the old gentleman went on. "Almost inevitably some of them paired off." Kempner no longer remembered the name of the manager, but judging by his description he could not have meant Baroness von Kleist, so another lady must have been in charge of the Witness House at the time.

Several more years passed before, in the mid-1990s, I went to Nuremberg. Twenty-four Novalisstrasse was the address of the villa given in the visitors' book. My first impression was disappointment. The house was small and low-built, a cube with a roof coming quite a long way down, and surrounded by a few tall pine trees—it looked plain and simple. Elisabeth Kühnle, an old lady of over eighty, opened the door to me. Wooden floorboards creaked as she led me into the living room, which was dominated by a massive sideboard polished to a high sheen. Judging by its design and color, it must have dated from before the war. White lace doilies were spread over various pieces of furniture, and there was also a radio that looked as if it had been in use for many years.

Elisabeth Kühnle was very chatty, her voice tinged with a Franconian accent. Yes, Baroness von Kleist had indeed been here in the old days, she said—"She always acted very grand, although her maiden name was only Müller or something like that." But before her, she confirmed, a countess had indeed run the place, a real aristocrat. "That was Countess Kálnoky," Frau Kühnle told me, and waxed enthusiastic. "What a woman! So beautiful, and a real lady." Countess Kálnoky, she said, had been the first manager of the two houses, and had later emigrated to the United States.

At the time of the Nuremberg trials Elisabeth Kühnle was not yet living in Novalisstrasse. The house had belonged to her aunt Elise Krülle. But young Frau Kühnle, newly married at the time, often came to visit, and so of course she had met Countess Kálnoky. Elise Krülle had died prematurely after the war, and her son Gerhard, who inherited the house, had sold it to his cousin Elisabeth. Countess Kálnoky had visited the new owner, and later she sent one or two postcards from America. After that, however, contact between them came to an end, and now the old lady in Nuremberg had no idea exactly where in the States the countess was to be found—if indeed she was still alive.

But in the winter of 1995 I rang Ingeborg Countess Kálnoky's doorbell. She was living in a suburb of Cleveland, Ohio, in a tiny apartment behind a huge shopping mall. I had managed to track down her address in old age through the Almanach de Gotha, the directory of the noble families of Europe. Her little living room was full of souvenirs. Boxes overflowing with crumpled pictures were scattered around, and there was a large framed photograph on a small table showing the Witness House in Novalisstrasse. There were stacks of yellowing letters of thanks, neatly tied up in bundles, and beside them a little brown book. The slightly greasy cover of this book, which was bound in a material that looked like linen, was adorned with three rhomboid shapes in different colors. Its pages must have been turned many times; they were almost coming apart. But the many signatures inside the book left me in no doubt: I was looking at another visitors' book from the Witness House at 24 Novalisstrasse, Nuremberg.

The little book reminded me of the kind of autograph album that young girls used to keep, and the countess herself, despite her advanced age, had preserved a remarkably youthful appearance. She sat very upright in her armchair, and a pearl necklace of several strands mingled with her shoulder-length white hair. She kept adjusting it with her long, carefully painted fingernails. Even now that she was eighty-seven, it was not difficult to see that she had once been an exceptionally beautiful woman. She had had many suitors, as I soon realized from the stories she told. But first the countess introduced me, in her husky voice and with a mischievous smile, to her present partner in life, a black cat called Russell.

We leafed through the visitors' book together, and Countess Kálnoky pointed out interesting names here and there. The first entry dated from October 1945, when Karl Haushofer, a former university professor who had taught Hitler's former deputy Rudolf Hess, stayed at the guesthouse. Haushofer's entry was grandiloquent and difficult to read. "We talked about subjects like reincarnation," the countess remembered, adding briefly: "He killed himself not long after his visit to the guesthouse." She still remembered the aircraft constructor Willy Messerschmitt vividly: "He said he'd invent a vacuum cleaner for us." Heinrich Hoffmann, Adolf Hitler's personal photographer, had been a frequent guest. "Shockingly superstitious," the old lady commented. "Once, when I opened an umbrella in his room just for fun, he was scared to death."

Hadn't there also been witnesses from the concentration camps? "Oh yes," said Kálnoky. "There was a farmer who'd been in Dachau—he darned socks for me." Groups of former concentration camp prisoners had stayed at the Witness House several times, she added, people who had been in Majdanek, Treblinka, or Mauthausen. At such times she had always been afraid, she added, that Hoffmann the photographer might sour the atmosphere. "He was so boastful," she said, adding that he was always denying the horrors of the Nazi period. "But would you believe it? When the concentration camp witnesses left, he exchanged addresses with them."

I stayed in Ohio for a few days to talk about all that the old lady could still remember in detail. In the evenings I was invited to the comfortable dining table of her daughter Lori Bongiovanni, whose full first name was Eleonora. She lived a few miles away in a beautiful house in the country with her husband, and came every day to make sure her mother was all right. Eleonora had been ten when Ingeborg Kálnoky took over the management of the Witness House. She still remembered details—for instance, the way the children used to enjoy spraying the GIs on sentry duty outside the two villas with water. Her younger brother Fárkas Kálnoky, whom I was to meet in Paris some years later, also retained childhood memories of Nuremberg. He recollected, for example, crawling around among the legs of no less than four real-life generals one Christmas Eve while he played battle with his new present, a set of toy soldiers.

The Witness House was obviously a place of opposites: pain and joy, laughter and tears, bitterness and arrogance in close proximity. Men and women whose recent experiences could not have been more different stayed there side by side. The past kept coming uncomfortably close to the present. The

Americans shielded the Witness House from questions and prying eyes. Hardly any of the many books that have been written about the Nuremberg trials even mention the villa in Novalisstrasse, although the Witness House was in use for over three years, from 1945 to 1948, and during that time well over a hundred witnesses stayed there. On the thirtieth anniversary of the beginning of the main trial, in 1975, the former manager of the Witness House, Ingeborg Countess Kálnoky, published a book herself, written with the aid of a ghostwriter. It came out in the United States under the title of *The Guest House.* In this work she describes, among other things, how the Americans gave her the job of managing the place. Her instructions were to "keep things running smoothly."

However, the incidents described in 1975 in *The Guest House* do not always agree with the account that Kálnoky wrote in the 1940s, when events in Nuremberg must have been fresh in her mind. Extracts from this earlier account were published in 1949 in a Munich newspaper. But even here the countess had not recorded everything, as I soon realized from my conversations with her and other contemporary witnesses. There was certainly a good deal that she could not have known at the time. After all, she did not manage the Witness House throughout its entire existence. But now and then I suspected that she did not *want* to record everything, and had skillfully glossed over certain incidents here and there.

So I began doing some more detailed research. I visited archives and tracked down other contemporary witnesses who were still alive to hear their version of events. Several years passed. I studied the transcripts of interrogations, as well as letters, diary entries, and first-person accounts, and found former guests of the Witness House who, curiously enough, had never entered their names in either of the two visitors' books.

Each of them provided me with new information and showed me a new point of view, and so, slowly, I formed an idea of the atmosphere in that unusual community brought together in the middle of Germany, in the immediate postwar period, through gentle pressure exerted by the Americans.

A GRANDE DAME TRAVELING LIGHT

There was a certain aura of gloom about the house, and yet it seemed very much more welcoming than anything Ingeborg Kálnoky had seen during the last few weeks. Its façade had an oddly patchwork appearance. Traveling-bag in hand, the young woman was standing outside it on a late August day in 1945, blinking into the morning sun. After all she had gone through, the little villa in the wood was like a safe haven that might at last offer her shelter. Yet at the same time she felt vaguely afraid of the new challenge ahead of her.

Inside the house, Elise Krülle was standing at the window, examining the new arrival with some suspicion. The countess was blonde, very blonde. Elise's son Gerhard, a bright boy of thirteen, was to remember her very clearly later: "She looked like Jean Harlow," he said. "The beautiful sinner type, you might say." The Krülle family's house, like the neighboring buildings in the street, had been camouflaged from air raids with splotches of brown and green paint. Whether it was thanks to these precautions, or to the rather remote situation of those buildings on the outskirts of the city, we cannot know, but here in the suburb of Erlenstegen they had remained relatively un-scathed by the bombs, although the Old Town of Nuremberg itself was reduced to rubble. There was nothing but ruins to be seen on the banks of the river Pegnitz, where half-timbered houses centuries old, adorned with fine carving, had collapsed into dust and ashes like sacks of flour slit open.

On the Krülle property, the only direct hit scored was on the garage. A few tiles had come off the roof of the house in the blast of bombs dropped farther away, some windowpanes had cracked, and bomb fragments had left a burn mark measuring about a square yard on the floor of one room on the second story of the house. All things considered, the damage had been relatively slight. That was good luck for the Krülles, but bad luck too, for the American occupying power immediately commandeered the house at 24 Novalisstrasse.

The Americans had arrived in the middle of April 1945, beginning with the combat troops. Later an administrative unit moved into the district on the eastern outskirts of Nuremberg. Elise Krülle had been keeping chickens and turkeys all through the war, so there was always enough to eat. But now the Yanks wrung the necks of chicken after chicken, plucked and skinned the fowl, and broiled them. They camped out in the Krülles' conjugal bedroom, and very soon created chaos out of the orderly household arrangements that Elise had doggedly kept going all through the war. They threw the picture of Hitler that used to hang in the living room out into the street and trampled on it. They scattered the family's stamp collection around the rooms and in the corridors. They found the black top hat in which Elise's husband had married her and used it as a target for shooting practice. The first impression that the Krülles gained of their American liberators was ambiguous, to say the least.

And now this blonde beauty was going to move in as well. Elise Krülle welcomed the stranger at the front door with proper civility, but she was not really very pleased to see her. In the last weeks of the war, Elise and her son had lived more or less entirely in the cellar. Now the two of them faced the possible threat of being driven out of their own home. The place was to be fitted out as a guesthouse; Elise Krülle, whose husband had been reported missing during the final days of the war, couldn't quite work out who was to be accommodated there, and now Ingeborg Countess Kálnoky was being shown around the top floor by the soldiers. The countess was uncomfortable with the idea that she was to choose a bedroom of her own here—even if it was only a small one—while the owner of the house and her son had to go on living in the cellar.

The young woman was suddenly prey to all kinds of doubts. Could she cope with the job she had been given? Would any of the women witnesses who were to stay in this house take her seriously? One of the officers who had brought her to Novalisstrasse seemed to notice her diffidence. "Ma'am," he assured her, "everyone will do exactly as you say, even Frau Göring—after all, you're the only countess around here."

Ingeborg Countess Kálnoky, née von Breitenbuch, now aged thirty-six, had arrived in Nuremberg only a few days before. But in that short time incident had followed incident in such swift succession that she felt a little dizzy. A short while ago she had been so hungry that she would have given anything for a few dry rolls of bread. Now she had a delicious hot meal from the American army canteen every day. There were clean linen sheets on the beds, and thick woolen blankets. It wasn't so long since Countess Kálnoky had been sleeping on a bare stone floor. In the old days, of course, everything had been different. Then she had lived in a wonderful castle in Transylvania—Köröspatak was its name, a white dream of a building, with roses climbing up the walls.

At the end of the 1930s, however, she, her husband, and their children had had to leave their beautiful home because

Transylvania was part of Romania, and the Romanians were allowing fewer and fewer Hungarian citizens to live there. Her husband, Hugo Count Kálnoky, who made a living now and then from translating Romanian newspaper articles into Hungarian, was accused of spying, and they had to leave the country within forty-eight hours. After that they stayed in Budapest for some time, but had to escape that city in haste as well in the spring of 1944, when the Gestapo turned up at the door of their apartment one day. Count Kálnoky was now working as an editor on the foreign desk of a German-language Budapest newspaper. His articles had also been broadcast to Germany on the BBC radio station, and that had alerted the Nazis to his activities. The bishop of Györ, also an aristocrat and a friend, had offered them temporary asylum, but it looked as if the Russians would soon march into Hungary, and in January 1945 the countess, with her three children and their nursemaid Cuci, set off on their way to the West. The countess suspected that she might be pregnant again.

They traveled by horse-drawn cart, in a stream of refugees, and by rail. Once, when they were on a train, fighter-bombers swooped low, and a German Wehrmacht soldier who was a fellow passenger tried firing at the airplanes from below. What a fool! Kálnoky immediately understood the danger and flung herself on the man. If she had not stopped him, bombs would very probably have hit the train, and all the passengers would have been blown sky-high with it. In Austria, Ingeborg Kálnoky first took refuge with her sister in Vienna, where the family was almost buried in rubble after an air raid. Later they fled on into Czechoslovakia, and reached a castle near Pilsen that belonged to other relations of theirs.

One day Kálnoky's eight-year-old son, Fárkas, who was in the castle courtyard, saw tanks rolling slowly up the hill. The tanks had stars painted on them, so it seemed more than likely that they were Russian. The family was hiding in the cellar of the building, terrified, when a group of soldiers stormed in. After a brief exchange of remarks, an officer offered the blonde countess a cigarette. It was a Camel; she still remembered this detail distinctly many years later. There was general relief—the man was American! For Countess Kálnoky, the war was over, but not her odyssey.

By this time the countess was in the ninth month of her pregnancy, and the baby could arrive any day. She urgently needed a hospital, preferably in Germany, to avoid falling into Russian hands. Thanks to the good offices of an American army doctor, she was finally moved from Pilsen to Nuremberg, although without her three children. The U.S. soldiers had taken the heavily pregnant woman, well protected by mattresses, away in a tank. Fárkas Kálnoky says he would still swear to that today. He and the other children stood waving as their mother disappeared in the armored vehicle.

Many years later I met Fárkas Kálnoky in Paris, where the count, then an elegant man in his late sixties, was living in an attractive suburb. A large portrait of his mother looked down on me as I sat on a delicate antique sofa, making notes of his memories. "Look at that picture," cried Kálnoky suddenly. "It's the living image of her!" We looked at the oil painting, which showed the countess at a time when Nuremberg was only just behind her: a beautiful woman with a very determined yet at the same time very appealing expression. "She was just like that!" repeated Kálnoky. "A grande dame who loved to make a grand entrance." At the same time, she was a woman who could always expect to get help and support.

The Americans took the expectant mother right into the city center of Nuremberg, where they stopped outside a building with a roof that still appeared to be intact. By means of gentle persuasion they induced the Franconian woman who owned the house to make a corner of her attic available to the countess. Her labor pains began one day in August, and thanks to her good relationship with the Americans, Kálnoky was even driven to the hospital in an army jeep. On August 15, 1945, Countess Kálnoky brought her fourth child into the world. It was a little girl.

Captain Kerr, a medical officer, had driven her to the hospital, which was run by a nursing order of nuns. A few days after the baby's birth, he came to the hospital again, this time with an army chaplain. The priest's dark hair was combed back, and he wore a pair of black-rimmed glasses. He too wore a captain's uniform. His name was Fabian Flynn, and the countess was never to forget him.

When the two Americans entered the hospital, a nun was just bringing in the baby. The two U.S. officers made themselves comfortable in the sickroom, put their feet up casually on a table, and kindly but firmly began asking the new mother questions. She was a Hungarian citizen, wasn't she? Kálnoky said she was, but explained that she was German by birth, that her parents lived at Ranis Castle in Thuringia, and that she herself had spent the last ten years with her husband in Hungary. Then she hadn't been in Germany during the Hitler period? That seemed to reassure Captain Kerr. She spoke English quite well, he went on—and presumably Hungarian too? "I speak English, French, German, and Hungarian," explained the countess, to which Kerr replied, as the countess remembered it: "Even better."

The captain continued his close questioning. At one point Father Flynn bent solicitously down to Kálnoky's bed. Did she know what she was going to do now? he asked. No, the countess really had no idea, she said, she didn't even know where her children were. There might be a chance of finding work for her, said the captain, joining in the conversation again, but his superior officer would have to make the decision. He'd arrange for her to meet the colonel the next day, said Captain Kerr. The priest patted the countess's hand again in a friendly manner, and then the men went away, leaving Ingeborg Kálnoky there in her bed feeling dazed, but with something to look forward to.

It took several more conversations, and Kálnoky had to undergo interrogation by an officer of the CIC, the American Counter Intelligence Corps, but then she landed the job. The countess was to run a guesthouse providing accommodation for the wives and other family members of the main war criminals, who were to be tried in Nuremberg very soon. Kálnoky had little time to decide whether she wanted to take the post, since she had to begin at once. There was no alternative but to leave her baby, born only a few days earlier, at the hospital. But first the child was to be christened, and she was given the name of Ingeborg, like her mother. Father Flynn conducted the christening service, the countess told me later during our conversations in Ohio. Then Kálnoky was driven to the house in the wood, with only a few bags. She still had no idea how much this step would change her life.

Elise Krülle proved more cooperative than expected. Elise, an energetic, dark-haired woman, was a trained tax inspector, but had almost never worked in that profession. However, she could keep accounts, and she was much too realistic and fond of life to close her mind to the new situation. Now aged fifty-one, she liked the young countess's lack of arrogance and her willingness to lend a hand herself. The two women shared another bond: anxiety about their husbands. By now Elise Krülle had little hope that her husband would ever come back—he had very probably fallen in Berlin in the closing days of the war, although there was still no confirmation. Countess Kálnoky had heard nothing from her own husband for months. Was he still in Hungary, was he even alive? She didn't know.

Soon the two women were working together to prepare the house for its future occupants. Beds and chairs were provided out of U.S. reserves. They were a motley collection, and many obviously came from confiscated household goods. Army employees delivered china and cutlery, towels, American woolen blankets, and linen sheets so wonderfully white and clean that even years later Kálnoky would go into ecstasies about them. Although the first GIs to enter the Krülles' house had ruined some of their things, the piano was still intact. It stood against a wall in the dining room. A bookcase in the study contained a rather old edition of *Meyer's Encyclopedia*, and a few of the works of Schiller. Furtively reading the encyclopedia, which was already rather well-worn, was soon to become a favorite occupation among the guests. Dipping into it was a good way to pass the time.

Ingeborg Kálnoky had moved into the house at the beginning of September 1945. Several more weeks were to pass before the first guests arrived. Meanwhile the countess's children had also been brought to Nuremberg. The Americans had smuggled them to the West hidden in an army truck, since the German-Czech border was already under Russian control. The three children could not move into Novalisstrasse until the officers responsible had given formal permission, so for now they went to stay with friends.

At this time there was much hectic activity all over Nuremberg in preparation for the beginning of the trial of the leading war criminals. The courthouse on Fürther Strasse, the Palace of Justice, was full of the sound of hammering and carpentry while prisoners of war, along with local craftsmen, were employed converting Courtroom 600, which was spacious, into a venue specially designed for the trials.

The Grand Hotel near the rail station, once Nuremberg's best hotel, underwent some makeshift repairs to accommodate lawyers and other guests expected at the opening of the main trial. This building, opposite the station, had been badly damaged by the air raids, but the Marble Room on the first floor was still usable. In the past, prosperous middle-class citizens had held wedding celebrations in it. Now jazz musicians would be performing here—but the waiters still wore tails. The Marble Room was soon considered a top destination by American society in Nuremberg. Few visitors to the Grand Hotel noticed that some of the fitted carpets on which they walked still had a swastika pattern woven into them.

Peace and quiet were also at an end in the Nuremberg suburb of Erlenstegen, where Novalisstrasse lay. The Americans had requisitioned whole rows of houses here. They were to be furnished for the judges, prosecutors, interpreters, and secretarial staff. The new occupants of these houses, as young Gerhard Krülle was quick to notice, never seemed to go hungry. When he walked around the streets of Erlenstegen in the fall of 1945, he saw large quantities of food being thrown into garbage cans. The locals used to come back quietly and take away anything that still seemed edible.

Meanwhile the Americans had changed their plans for the Novalisstrasse house. Instead of accommodating the wives of the main defendants, the small villa in the wood was now designated a guesthouse where witnesses summoned by the court, or by the prosecution at least, could stay while they were in Nuremberg. Ingeborg Kálnoky was relieved to hear this news, for she had hated the idea of having to exchange small talk on a daily basis with women like Emmy Göring. She did not know yet, of course, what a difficult time she would have keeping happy all the very different guests who were now expected. In the end witnesses for both the prosecution and the defense stayed at the little villa—which meant that former Nazis and members of the Resistance were under the same roof.

The Allies had prepared various different quarters for the witnesses in the trials. A special wing of the prison was attached to the courthouse for those witnesses who came from Allied internment camps, or whom it seemed advisable to keep in custody because they were under suspicion themselves. In the fall of 1945 this wing also provided temporary accommodation for some of the defendants' wives, women who had previously been destined for Novalisstrasse. Not far from the courthouse building, at 2a Muggenhofer Strasse, another building was converted into temporary accommodation for those witnesses who had not come from prison camps, and were officially allowed to move freely—although it did not always work out like that in practice.

The house in Novalisstrasse was also to take some of these "voluntary" witnesses, as they were called. However, it soon turned out that their liberty of movement was only relative. GI guards were stationed at the entrance at certain times to check that no one left the house without permission. Many of those who stayed there went straight to prison when they left the guesthouse on the outskirts of the wood. Other guests who had come from internment camps were formally considered free, but a discreet watch was kept on them. Some of the important witnesses for the prosecution were even given bodyguards for their own protection; others were under room arrest for reasons that hardly anyone understood.

But at the same time the guests' stay at the house was to be made as comfortable as possible. After all, some very prominent people were expected. Few guesthouses for the witnesses in the old city on the Pegnitz were as exclusive in those days as the Novalisstrasse villa. At first the defense lawyers were also very keen to be allowed to stay there. Besides the Krülle family's house at number 24, number 25 was also available, although it consisted only of sleeping quarters. Meals were eaten together in the main house, where social life also took place. Countess Kálnoky was to manage the house; Elise Krülle was to help her as chambermaid and waitress.

As her first guest, Ingeborg Kálnoky welcomed a broken old man with a high forehead and watery blue eyes, Professor Karl Haushofer, once the university tutor of Rudolf Hess, who was later the Führer's deputy. He was also regarded as the man who had inspired Hitler's policy of Lebensraum, although he had later fallen into disfavor with the Führer. Haushofer arrived at the Witness House at the end of September 1945. Everything about the old man, now seventy-six years old, seemed sad to the countess. He looked "remote from the world and tired," as she noted at the time.

Almost from the day she began her job in Novalisstrasse, Ingeborg Kálnoky had a strong feeling that she was taking part in a historic event. She did not keep a diary in the usual sense of the word, but during the 1940s she typed an account of around 140 pages and let some of the guests read it. As a title for her record of events, one of the guests at the Witness House suggested "In the Shadow of Nemesis," and the text does indeed have the emotion conveyed by that title. However, her observations are sometimes rather one-sided. There were witnesses whom Kálnoky never mentioned, although it can be proved that they stayed in Novalisstrasse. On the other hand, she devoted several pages to descriptions of other witnesses who were never of any noticeable importance at the trials or in any other way. All the same, the countess's personal account does contain very useful hints for a researcher, and makes some cogent points—Kálnoky was looking at her guests in a "strictly private" way, as she phrases it in the subtitle of her document.

One of those was old Haushofer, whom she obviously liked. He had been an army officer in the First World War, like her own father, and later became a professor of geopolitics. In 1916, while he was in the army, Haushofer had traveled through Transylvania, and may well have seen Köröspatak Castle at that time. So there was plenty for him to talk to the countess about while he waited to give evidence. He was to be interrogated by Edmund A. Walsh, a well-known Jesuit priest and political economist who taught at Georgetown University in Washington, D.C.

Haushofer interested the prosecutors for two reasons: first, because his geopolitical ideas had served as a theoretical basis for Hitler's belligerent policy of expansion, and second, because he had been in close contact over a long period with his former student Hess. As Haushofer's philosophical system saw it, only the major nations were capable of survival, and smaller countries must necessarily go under. Germany, he thought, was destined to play a crucial part in Europe, and he considered Japan predestined to assume the same role in Asia. In practice, then, the professor had helped to forge the wartime alliance between Japan and the Third Reich.

At first the authorities had considered prosecuting the archreactionary university teacher himself. But the old man with the Hindenburg mustache could not be shown to have taken any part in the real preparations for war, and he was able to show credibly that he had fallen out of favor with Hitler as early as 1938. In addition, he had a weak heart, and he seemed to have suffered enough already from his family's fate. His son Albrecht Haushofer, a geographer and writer, had joined the Resistance circle around Carl Friedrich Goerdeler in the 1940s. He was arrested after the assassination attempt on Hitler's life of July 20, 1944, and later shot. Haushofer senior had himself spent several weeks in the Dachau concentration camp because of his son's activities.

Father Walsh sat in the study of the Witness House with the professor and questioned him over several days, but apparently no important information came to light. The old man defended his geopolitical visions as the outcome of the devastating situation in which Germany had found itself in 1919, soon after the end of the First World War, when the Treaty of Versailles allowed no scope for expansion. However, he said, that had nothing to do with Hitler's Lebensraum policy. He also strongly denied having ever contributed to the writing of Hitler's *Mein Kampf*, that fundamental treatise of National Socialism, which had set out the ideas behind most of the later Nazi crimes. And he claimed that he had never received a penny from the Nazis.

Between interrogations, the old man had to keep stopping to rest. He had already suffered two heart attacks during his stay at the Witness House, so he spent long hours in the garden with the countess, petting Elise Krülle's kitten, which liked to sit on his lap. Then he would suddenly come out with musings on guilt and atonement. "Even if it was a very long time before people had any idea of Hitler's diabolical tactics, one does somehow feel guilty too," he said in remorseful tones one day from his deck chair. The countess wrote down this remark.

HITLER'S PERSONAL PHOTOGRAPHER,
OR HOW TO GET BY

———————

Someone was ringing the doorbell loudly and insistently. Peering through the kitchen window, Elise Krülle saw an American ambulance. She opened the front door of the house, and the next moment the visitors were making their way into the hall. A U.S. soldier was escorting two men who seemed to be in rather bad shape. They were unshaven, and the smaller of them wore garments that made him look like a typical Bavarian country bumpkin: a battered Tyrolean hat, a rather well-worn jacket in the traditional style, and a pair of striped pants from a business suit, which were obviously much too large for him and were held up by a thin leather belt.

The American soldier turned to the countess, saying in English, "Tell these gentlemen they're free, please." Then he put his hand into the pocket of his uniform coat and brought out a wallet. He handed both men a few bills and said good-bye. The taller man took the money rather hesitantly; the smaller one grabbed it eagerly. He carefully counted the bills again, folded them up, and stuffed the thin bundle of paper into his pocket. "Getting your money back," he remarked, well satisfied, as he nudged his still rather diffident companion, "is the surest sign that you're out of prison."

Then he finally turned to the countess. "Good day to you, ma'am," he said with an awkward gesture simulating the kissing of a lady's hand. "Allow me to introduce myself: Heinrich Hoffmann, professor of fine arts." The second new arrival, who wore an army jacket with the epaulets cut off, also introduced himself: "Dr. Wilhelm Scheidt, cavalry captain in the reserve troops." The two men came from different prison camps, and through the little windows of the ambulance they had been unable to see where they were heading. Hoffmann had been afraid of being taken to the Russian zone. It was true that he had "once drunk a toast to friendship with Stalin," as he proudly told the countess later that evening—but you never knew what the Russians might think of you these days.

Heinrich Hoffmann had been Hitler's personal photographer. By dint of wily business acumen rather than his photographic skills, he had practically cornered the market in photographs of Hitler. He had taken the public portrait of the Führer. Whenever and wherever photographs of Hitler were published, as a general rule they had been taken by Heinrich Hoffmann. He had acquired considerable wealth through his privileged position as the Führer's photographer. Originally starting out with a small photographic studio in Schwabing, the bohemian quarter of Munich, by the early forties he had over three hundred employees, with branches of his business in all the German-occupied areas, and he was a multimillionaire.

At the end of the war, like many others who had been prominent during the Nazi period, Hoffmann found himself in a prison camp. Now the Americans had brought the photographer to Nuremberg to sort through his extensive photographic archive for them. Thousands of his pictures had been confiscated, and could be important contemporary documentation if produced in court as evidence. The photos showed the dictator and his close circle in many different groupings, and such pictures could show exactly who had been in the Führer's company and when. Many of the accused were now claiming that they had known Hitler only very little, if at all—the pictures often told a different story.

Hoffmann had a talent for always turning everything to his own advantage, and he soon saw how to profit from his new situation in Nuremberg. On their first evening he and the German officer who had traveled with him made a very dejected impression on the countess. They sat at supper in the Witness House with the sad figure of Haushofer, and no one managed to start a lively conversation of the kind the countess enjoyed. At this point Hoffmann still had no idea what he was there for, and Scheidt, who had been a high-ranking officer in the Wehrmacht supreme command, was haunted by vague fears that the Americans might consider him a war criminal. As for Haushofer the geopolitician, he was lost in melancholy thought as usual. The countess, at any rate, registered a general mood of depression around the table.

The very next day, however, Hoffmann seemed a man transformed. Kálnoky saw him coming back from the courthouse in good humor that afternoon, an American cigarette in his mouth, and under his arm a bundle of papers, including some drawings and comic verses. He had begun a thriving trade in the courthouse building selling drawings of nudes to the GIs and sometimes, perhaps, a picture of Hitler. In return the Americans gave him cigarettes, soap, coffee, and whisky—all the things that were scarce and therefore very valuable at that time. Soon his room looked like a warehouse. U.S. soldiers went in and out of the Witness House to barter goods with Hoffmann. Haushofer and the army officer Scheidt, a rather stout middle-aged man, found all this rather tasteless. "Some people always fall on their feet," remarked Haushofer one evening, disapprovingly.

Hoffmann couldn't understand the attitude of the other two; the only values he appeared to recognize were of a material nature. If the discussion at meals touched on the present situation in Germany, and the rest of the company started wondering which of their old acquaintances might still be in internment camps, he took no interest. All he wanted to know was what there was to eat and where to find it. Scheidt, who obviously liked to appear remorseful about the Nazi past, pointed out that at the Witness House they could consider themselves lucky. Elsewhere people were living in cellars, went hungry, and had to stand in line even for a few quarts of drinking water. Here, on the other hand, they were very well fed and lodged.

"No false modesty, Captain," replied Hoffmann. "We're doing something to earn our keep." Then the photographer explained the preparations for the trials now going on as he himself saw them. "It's obvious why the Yanks are splurging on us—we're witnesses, and you can't have a trial without witnesses."

The Bavarian also liked to boast of his close contact with Hitler. He, Hoffmann, was apparently the only friend who could gain access to the Führer at any time of day or night—and the Führer, he said, also used to visit him. Back in the old days in Munich, Hitler sometimes used to call on Hoffmann in his apartment late in the evening and would sit in an armchair by the fire listening to his stories. Sometimes he dropped off to sleep, said the photographer. However, Hitler had obviously always felt at ease in his company, and on leaving he often thanked him with the words: "Hoffmann, you're the only one among them who doesn't pester me."

Hitler and the photographer had met in 1923, and clearly their friendship had lasted until the end of the war. Hoffmann had joined the National Socialist Party early; his membership card bore the low number 56. At first Hitler had been decidedly camera-shy, he said, and he, Hoffmann, had to exert much persuasion before he finally got him in front of his lens. After that, however, Hitler had been his most loyal photographic model. In April 1945 Hoffmann went to the Führer's bunker in Berlin to say good-bye to the dictator, by then only a shadow of his former self. For those reasons, in the fall of that year the Americans had the impression that a very good source of information on Hitler had fallen into their hands in the shape of the photographer. "Knows more than anyone about Hitler," someone noted in a file on Hoffmann.

At the Witness House, of course, the photographer never tired of saying that his relationship with Hitler had been "entirely nonpolitical." Or at least, he assured all and sundry, they had never discussed politics or any serious problems. It was he who had introduced Hitler to Eva Braun, who would become the dictator's wife at the very end. Eva Braun had been employed in the Munich branch of Hoffmann's business, where the photographic entrepreneur sorted out his postcards and sent them off for distribution. Hoffmann's opinion of his former employee, with whom he may well have had a fleeting relationship himself at one time, did not, however, seem very high. "Easy on the eye, but no intellectual qualities" was his verdict on Hitler's mistress.

The photographer had an inexhaustible fund of anecdotes, and as a result the "Tales of Hoffmann" were soon a byword in the Witness House. Elise Krülle became one of the most faithful of his audience. Hoffmann would sit in her kitchen for hours on end, telling stories of what had apparently been the good old days. The photographer had been well-known in Nuremberg during the Nazi period. Hoffmann, now sixty years old, came from neighboring Fürth, and he used to turn up with Hitler at the Party rallies year after year, later publishing handsome picture books illustrating them. These volumes bore such titles as *The Unknown Side of Hitler* or *Hitler Builds the Greater German Reich*. Elise Krülle, who had certainly swallowed a good deal of Nazi propaganda, might well have had one of them in her bookcase in the past, along with *Meyer's Encyclopedia* and Schiller's play *Wallenstein*. At any rate, she liked listening to Hoffmann's nonstop flow of talk, and her son Gerhard also listened to these performances now and then.

Gerhard Krülle had been in the Hitler Youth, and had felt youthful enthusiasm for the Führer. At first, the boy took the end of the war and the arrival of the Americans as a heavy defeat. Some time before the Witness House was opened, however, a newspaper fell into the thirteen-year-old's hands. Later, he could not remember whether it was one of the newly licensed German news sheets or an American newspaper in the German language, but one page of it remained firmly rooted in his mind. Gerhard had picked up the newspaper somewhere in the street. At home he had climbed behind the ruined wall of the bombed-out garage and sat down on the grass there to read it undisturbed.

The newspaper contained photographs, dreadful photographs, from the concentration camps. The accompanying text described the unspeakable horrors of which the Nazis had been guilty. Gerhard read the report twice, three times. He felt profoundly disillusioned. He had thought of Hitler as a father figure, the man who had made sure that Germany counted for something in the world. Whether at school or in the parental home, he had heard nothing but praise of the Führer for years. Gerhard's own father, Walter Krülle, missing for many months now, had even volunteered for the army out of his conviction that the Nazi cause was just, although at nearly fifty he was past the age for military service in action.

They had all worked hard for Hitler. Gerhard Krülle could hardly believe what he was reading. His idol had been a criminal, and many of his fellow countrymen had also been guilty of terrible crimes. Reading that article was a key experience for the thirteen-year-old, and he was never to forget sitting down with the newspaper behind the garage wall. Even sixty years later, when I visited him in 2005, the now-retired professor remembered every detail of that moment of revelation.

We sat in his comfortable home, with climbing plants lovingly entwined around the window frames, and I listened to the rest of the story. After the war, Gerhard Krülle studied mechanical engineering, and then moved into research on space flight. He made a career first in industry, then as a scientist and university lecturer. It may be that behind that garage wall in Nuremberg, as he later believed, he had something like a revelation, a dismal certainty that it would take the Germans generations to come to terms with their guilt. This remarkably farsighted view on the part of a boy of thirteen may also have affected his observations of what was going on in Novalisstrasse.

The young Gerhard saw some of the comings and goings at the Witness House. He picked up snatches of conversation, watched the GIs and the U.S. officers who came to the house every day, and he instinctively pricked up his ears when a discussion became heated. As if incidentally, Gerhard Krülle picked up more and more English words in this way. He also noticed how affectionate relationships began to develop between some of those who worked in or visited the house. He saw, for instance, that Elli, the young woman who helped out in the kitchen, was involved with a GI. The man was a "rough diamond" from Arkansas, as Krülle still remembers, and delivered the food for the house daily in a U.S. jeep. In fact it was hard to be sure whether it was really Elli the soldier was after or her fourteen-year-old daughter. The boy watched with interest as the GI pulled the girl down on his lap, saying cheerfully: "C'm on, sit on Papa's knee."

Supplies were driven to Novalisstrasse three times a day, in huge green army cooking pans. Inside, the tiny kitchen to the right of the front door was under the command of Frau Kreisel, a robust, rather stout middle-aged woman. The food delivered by the Americans seemed strange to the German palate. For breakfast, besides fried eggs and grilled bacon, there was grapefruit juice and peanut butter—nothing like that had ever been seen in Nuremberg. The coffee was weak, but at least there *was* coffee. And by the standards of the time, the size of the portions was very generous.

At first there were not too many guests to be looked after. Hoffmann and Scheidt had arrived on October 3, 1945. Just under a week later, Karl Haushofer left. Before that, a meeting had been arranged between him and his former student Rudolf Hess, who had just been transferred from Great Britain to Nuremberg. The Führer's former deputy seemed mentally confused, and claimed to be unable to remember anything. To jog his memory, the prosecutors tried confronting him with acquaintances from his past.

However, not much came of his encounter with Haushofer. The old professor had always kept in touch with his former students, and presumably had been protected by Hess from the effects of Nazi racial policy, for Haushofer's wife was half Jewish. Hitler's deputy had spoken to Haushofer only a little while before making his secret flight to Scotland in May 1941. It seems likely that the unauthorized action taken by Hess, when, failing entirely to recognize the true situation, he hoped to start peace negotiations with Britain, had also been discussed with the professor's son Albrecht Haushofer, for the latter was then arrested for the first time. However, it was Haushofer's impression at this confrontation with Rudolf Hess in October 1945 that Hess really did not recognize him, and indeed the Führer's former deputy seemed to Haushofer himself like a stranger. The old man, melancholy enough anyway, returned to the Witness House seeming even more despondent after this meeting, according to the countess's account.

Meanwhile a visitor had arrived whom Elise Krülle, and the rest of the domestic staff, were soon to be seeing more often. This was the army chaplain Fabian Flynn, who had visited the countess in the hospital just after she had had her baby. As Haushofer noted later in a letter, Father Flynn looked in at the Witness House with a colonel—possibly one of those U.S. officers who had appointed Countess Kálnoky to her post. The two Americans seemed to be good friends, and the countess was obviously pleased to see them, as Haushofer noted. In his letter, the professor mentioned that the chaplain had taken a "very kindly interest" in the mistress of the house.

Fabian Flynn was a good-looking U.S. officer, aged forty, and no one would necessarily have taken him for a man of the cloth at first sight. He normally wore an ordinary uniform jacket; he was tall and well built, and looked fit. Only the cross on his lapel showed that he was a priest. Flynn had been at the front during the war. His personal files record periods spent in North Africa and Sicily, and he was in Normandy on D-day. Father Flynn worked sometimes in field hospitals, sometimes directly at the front, and he had also been involved now and then in active military operations. He had been severely wounded at the end of 1944.

The Catholic priest now held the rank of captain, and he had received many decorations for his courage in action, some of which he wore on his uniform, including the Silver Star, a major American award for bravery. In civil life Fabian Flynn, a member of the Catholic order the Congregation of the Passion, or the Passionists, lived in a monastery in Boston, but he never stayed there for long. In the spring of 1945, as soon as he had recovered from his injury, he had himself transferred back to the combat troops. And so a few months later Flynn and his unit, the 26th Infantry Regiment of the U.S. Third Army, reached the city of Nuremberg, which had been devastated by the air raids. The regiment was soon to have an important job on its hands in helping to prepare for the war crimes trials, and Flynn himself was also involved in working for the military tribunal in a number of ways.

The priest visited POW camps and hospitals. At the end of August 1945, Fabian Flynn had also been appointed official chaplain to the American war crimes commission. That brought the Witness House into his sphere of competence. The document relating to his appointment, consisting of an informal note signed by a major, shows that the 26th Infantry also had an arrangement with the countess, so it was taken for granted that she would turn to the priest with her anxieties now and then.

And she had a problem. So far, the U.S. authorities had not allowed Countess Kálnoky's children to be with her at the Witness House. Naturally the countess wanted nothing more, and she managed to get permission. It is not known whether the priest helped or whether it was settled with other assistance. In the late fall of 1945, however, the three older children, Eleonora, Fàrkas, and Antal, and baby Ingeborg, who had been born on August 15, moved to Novalisstrasse, along with their nursemaid Cuci. From now on the atmosphere in the house was rather livelier.

Fabian Flynn regularly visited Novalisstrasse. He showed such warm concern for the welfare of the lady of the house that Elise Krülle and many of the rest of the staff observed his visits with particular interest. However, the countess never said a word about the priest later in her own account of that time, nor is there any mention of Fabian Flynn in her book *The Guest House*, published in 1975.

The Witness House itself called for the countess's whole attention. A phone call from the Palace of Justice one day informed her that a new guest would be coming, one for whom special measures obviously had to be taken. Kálnoky was told to reserve a spacious room in the main house for him. The next day two military policemen delivered the man to Novalisstrasse. He was in his mid-forties, tall and well built, with very black hair and unusually blue eyes. There was a long scar down his left cheek, a dueling scar from his student days.

The stranger introduced himself as Rudolf Diels, took the countess's hand, and, with perfect manners, planted a kiss on it. Kálnoky was enchanted. In a cheerful mood, she took the new arrival to a large room with a balcony on the second floor, once the conjugal bedroom of the Krülles. There one of the U.S. escorts told her that the man was not allowed to leave his room—"He's under room arrest," the soldier explained. "No one's to see him, and he's not to talk to anyone."

This did surprise the lady of the house, but she assumed that the two military policemen were going to guard the stranger themselves. The next moment, however, they turned to go. She looked with some irritation first at her new guest, who was a good six feet tall, then at the Americans. "You expect *me* to guard him?" It would be enough to lock the door and take the key away with her, one of the soldiers explained, but then added sternly, "You are responsible!"

Ingeborg Kálnoky looked incredulously at the Americans, but the captive suddenly spoke up himself. "Dear lady, I promise to be an extremely docile prisoner," he said, unabashed. He paused, and then gave the lady of the house a mischievous smile. "I can't think of anything more delightful than to be in the custody of such a charming guard." Ingeborg Kálnoky blushed. Her new guest obviously thought himself irresistible.

Over the next few days, the countess carried food up to his room three times a day, and Diels always managed to involve her in a short conversation. There was a large double bed in the Krülles' bedroom, and a small table where Diels usually sat playing solitaire. A large pitcher of water and a basin had been placed in the room for him, so that he could freshen up without leaving it. If he needed anything, Diels knocked on the floor with a walking stick, and he could be heard in the study downstairs. Now and then one of the U.S. counterespionage service, the CIC, came to collect him. Rudolf Diels always seemed pleased, as if it was a relief to be allowed to leave his room.

The countess still had no idea just who her mysterious guest was. But the loquacious photographer was soon to enlighten her. One evening, as she was carrying a tray upstairs, he asked, grinning, if there was room service in the house now. "Room arrest is the word for it, I think," replied Kálnoky promptly, and told Hoffmann about the new guest. When he heard the name Diels he whistled softly though his teeth. "I thought he was dead."

Then he told the countess about the new arrival, at some length. "That's the founder of the Gestapo you have under room arrest here."

THE PROSECUTOR AND
THE GESTAPO CHIEF

A croaking voice came from the big radio set on the sideboard. There was an atmosphere of lively interest in the study of the Witness House. Scheidt the Wehrmacht officer was there, along with some guests who had arrived over the previous few days. They were all sitting on assorted armchairs and upright chairs at the round table, listening to a broadcast from Berlin, where the indictment for the trial of the principal war criminals was being presented, on October 18, 1945.

Matters were getting serious. The Allies had originally supported the proposition to make Berlin the official location for the proceedings of the tribunal in order to oblige the Russians, who wanted all the court hearings to be held in the former Reich capital. But the Americans strongly objected to holding the main trial in the Russian zone of occupation, which included large parts of Berlin. Finally everyone agreed on Nuremberg, which was under American control. The trial of the leading war criminals was to begin on November 20, 1945.

The indictment ran to over eighty typewritten pages, and named twenty-four defendants. Some of the National Socialist organizations considered by the Allies to be criminal in themselves were also indicted, including the Reich government, the SS, and the Gestapo. Among the defendants were such

National Socialist grandees as Hermann Göring and Rudolf Hess; the former foreign minister of the Reich, Joachim von Ribbentrop; Walther Funk, the economics minister and president of the Reich Bank; the military officers Wilhelm Keitel, Alfred Jodl, and Erich Raeder; and the last head of government of the Third Reich, Grand Admiral Karl Dönitz. Almost all the accused had been transferred to the prison wing of the Nuremberg courthouse building. The Witness House itself had filled up in the days before the trial began. Many lawyers had arrived. "The defense counsel," as the countess noted, "almost all stayed at this house."

Rudolf Dix was one of the first to arrive. He was a highly regarded criminal lawyer, with a fine head of snow-white hair. Dix had traveled from Berlin to Nuremberg, where he met his colleague from Göttingen, Herbert Kraus, a lean, gray-haired attorney who had a high reputation. The two lawyers had said they were prepared to undertake the defense of a former president of the Reich Bank, Hjalmar Schacht. Soon two more lawyers arrived at the Witness House: Hermann Jahreiss of Dresden and Franz Exner of Munich, a professor of law. They had both taken on the defense of Colonel General Jodl, Hitler's personal field strategist and chief of staff of the Wehrmacht. Finally, Walter Siemers and Viktor von der Lippe, counsel for Grand Admiral Raeder, arrived from Hamburg.

There was much discussion in the evenings at the Witness House in these days. Individual lawyers were anxious to explain to themselves and everyone else why, while they definitely did not want it to be thought that they were defending the old regime, they were representing their respective clients. "Defending a man accused of a crime," reasoned Raeder's counsel von der Lippe, was to be seen as "a professional task for a lawyer, similar to a physician's duty to provide medical aid." Others did not feel it necessary to justify themselves—they regarded the charges as a case of victors' justice, which, as patriotic Germans, they must oppose. A number of the attorneys had themselves been sympathetic to the National Socialist Party in the recent past, or had even been Party members; others principally wanted to be there because the trial promised to be an extraordinary historical event.

Both the number of Nazi crimes as they gradually became known during the trial and the extent of their atrocity had assumed dimensions barely comprehensible by ordinary human standards. The guests staying at the Witness House reacted in different ways. Some closed their eyes to the revelations, denied and suppressed them; others felt overwhelmed by the burden of guilt. Others again feared ending up on the defendants' bench themselves, which made them increasingly nervous.

Wilhelm Scheidt, of the Wehrmacht High Command (the OKW, short for Oberkommando Wehrmacht), had been waiting in the Witness House for weeks to be interrogated, but no one wanted to talk to him. Once, in November 1945, the Americans asked him to make a declaration under oath about the opposition of the Wehrmacht and the SS to partisans—a very delicate subject. But then Scheidt heard no more from the U.S. officers, so he had nothing to do but examine his memory again and again: did he have any cause to reproach himself?

Scheidt had worked in the department of war history at the Wehrmacht High Command and had kept the records of the army general staff in order. In that capacity, when his superior officer, General Walter Scherff, was injured during the assassination attempt at the Führer's headquarters on July 20, 1944, Scheidt had taken part in Hitler's discussions of the situation in the Wolf's Lair, a bunker complex at Rastenburg in Masuria. At the Witness House, Scheidt told the countess that he himself had been a member of the military Resistance to Hitler, but he guessed that the Americans were not going to believe him. Meanwhile the prosecutors left him to stew in his own juice—they had other priorities.

The indictment drawn up in Berlin comprised four principal charges. The twenty-four defendants were accused of engaging in a conspiracy against peace. The word *Verschwörung*, the German translation of the English "conspiracy," is a very general term. It is so general that, as many of the attorneys feared, it might also cover some rather vague accusations. Furthermore, the defendants were accused of taking part in the planning and conduct of a war of aggression. They were also accused of a whole range of serious war crimes carrying penalties as contraventions of the Hague Commission on the laws of warfare on land, and of the Geneva Convention of 1929. Finally, the defendants were accused of crimes against humanity, such as the persecution and methodical annihilation of the Jewish population.

Hardly any of those staying at the Witness House at this time ventured to cast doubt on the fact that terrible things had indeed happened during the Nazi period. However, many of the defending counsel thought that holding individuals responsible for them now was a dubious principle. One lawyer who expressed his opinion with particular eloquence was Otto Kranzbühler, a very good-looking man, still quite young, who was to defend Admiral Dönitz. Kranzbühler had himself been an officer on active service with the navy, and behind the front line had been a naval judge. He always appeared in smart naval uniform at the Witness House, not least as a visible reminder that he was still in the navy. He had merely been doing his duty, as he saw it, and he took on the defense of his client Dönitz in that spirit.

Countess Kálnoky had instructions to let the lawyers stay at the Witness House for as short a time as possible, since the

Allies, after all, were not responsible for the accommodation of the defense team. Rudolf Dix soon found somewhere else to stay, and scrawled his thanks for the "delightful hospitality" of the house in the visitors' book, leaving a large ink blob behind. Kranzbühler too was expected to leave what he had found a "pleasantly well-heated house." He sounds almost melancholy writing in the visitors' book, on November 6, 1945, "I am very sorry to leave this hospitable home."

The young lawyer was soon to make a name for himself with the precision and rigor of his defense of his clients, both in the main trial and the secondary trials that followed. The Witness House remained in his memory as "a very plush place for the circumstances of that time." On leaving it, Kranzbühler moved into a bomb-damaged room that "could be reached only up a henhouse ladder," as he told me many years later.

By the time I met him, Kranzbühler was an old man of eighty-eight, living in an attractive house beside the Tegernsee lake, but he could still easily enumerate the motley collection of guests he had encountered in Novalisstrasse back in those days, both during his own stay at the Witness House and later when he went there to meet witnesses. He had vivid memories not only of Hoffmann the photographer but of his daughter Henriette von Schirach, wife of the former Nazi Gauleiter of Vienna, Baldur von Schirach, one of the defendants in Nuremberg. She always stayed at the Witness House when she came to Nuremberg, although presumably only after the spring of 1946, since before that she was still interned. While the father conducted his deals with the GIs, the daughter flirted outrageously with some of the U.S. officers, as Kranzbühler remembered with a grin. She was "a very chic woman," he said, with glossy red-brown hair.

Otto Kranzbühler also had tales to tell of Fritz Wiedemann, Hitler's former adjutant. Wiedemann, an army officer and a diplomat, may therefore have been at the Witness House in the fall of 1945, although the countess does not mention him in her account. In fact Wiedemann's signature appears only many months later, in the second visitors' book, begun by Baroness von Kleist when she took over the management of the Witness House. However, a declaration made under oath to the Americans shows that Wiedemann was in Nuremberg in November 1945.

Fritz Wiedemann, born in 1891, had been one of Hitler's first devotees. The two had met in 1915, when the man who was to be the Führer had been Wiedemann's orderly during the First World War. Wiedemann was regimental adjutant in the 16th Bavarian Reserve Infantry Regiment at the time. Later, Hitler made Wiedemann his own adjutant in the Reich Chancellery. However, the first differences of opinion between them arose in 1938, as a result, said Wiedemann in 1945, of a meeting of Nazi grandees that included Göring, Ribbentrop, and Keitel, at which Hitler had made it very clear that he intended to go to war.

"It is my firm resolve to wipe Czechoslovakia off the map," the Führer had stated, as Wiedemann remembered it, on May 28, 1938. From that day on, Wiedemann told the American officers who interrogated him in November 1945, it had been clear to him that Hitler was bent on war. Wiedemann claimed to have tried to warn the British through diplomatic channels. In January 1939 he was moved from Hitler's close circle to the Foreign Ministry, going first to San Francisco as consul general, and later to Tientsin in China.

At the Witness House in Nuremberg, "Captain Wiedemann," as Kranzbühler called him, was under the personal protection of Robert M. W. Kempner, regarded as one of the most important members of the American prosecution. Kempner was also, according to Kranzbühler's observations, protecting another of the visitors who stayed at the Witness House: the former Gestapo chief Rudolf Diels, the man whom the countess was supposed to keep under room arrest.

Kempner was famous for his interrogations, in which he would use his own inimitable mixture of easy friendliness and unmistakable threats to get those he was questioning to talk—and when preparations for the trial were going on in Nuremberg, there can hardly have been an American who knew more about the leaders of the Third Reich than Kempner. Born in Freiburg im Breisgau in 1899, he had worked in the police department of the Prussian Ministry of the Interior in Berlin in the 1930s. It was there that he had come to know Diels, also a lawyer.

Before the Nazis came to power, the two men used to meet frequently in the ministry canteen, and later at least once in the well-known restaurant of the Kempinski Hotel in Berlin. This connection may have saved Kempner's life. He had himself once extricated Diels from a difficult situation, so they both had good reason to show gratitude. At the beginning of the 1930s Diels, born in 1900, had been initially responsible for the observation and countering of Communist movements, working under Carl Severing, a Social Democratic politician and at the time interior minister of Prussia. In April 1933, when the Nazis had come to power all over the country, the Prussian minister president and now interior minister Hermann Göring had given Diels the job of heading the newly created Secret State Police (the Geheimes Staatspolizeiamt) in Berlin, the Gestapo.

Shortly before this, however, his weakness for beautiful women had almost cost the lawyer his job. One morning in the early 1930s Rudolf Diels asked Kempner for help. The night before, said Diels, he had quarreled with a lady of easy virtue, and he had, unfortunately, left his personal pass at her home. He was sure the girl would go to the ministry at some point to sully his reputation. Sure enough, a young woman did turn up at the reception desk quite soon, wanting to speak to the minister. Kempner made sure that she was brought to him instead, and when she showed him Diels's pass, complaining that her client had beaten her up, Kempner simply pocketed the pass and paid the girl a small sum to keep her mouth shut.

In February 1933 Kempner lost his post as a legal adviser to the police. Like so many other Jewish civil servants, he had been fired. A little later, at the Kempinski Hotel, Diels told him about a list of persons to be arrested, including all kinds of "former friends." Kempner's name was not on the list. Diels, Kempner remained convinced, would "never have done" such a thing as to put him on it. A little later the Reichstag building burned down, and the first result was a wave of arrests. Kempner was in time to warn several of those who had been on the list drawn up by Diels, but many others were unable to escape the power of the state.

Two years later, in 1935, Kempner was arrested. At this point Diels was no longer in Berlin. He had handed in his resignation as head of the Gestapo in the spring of 1934, and Göring had been happy to accept it. In his power struggle with the SS chief Heinrich Himmler, the Prussian interior minister found Diels useful as a pawn who could be sacrificed, and Himmler's close friend Reinhard Heydrich took over as chief of the Gestapo. However, Göring had a weakness for Diels, and did not want to abandon the young civil servant entirely; he made him head of the administrative district of Cologne. Kempner's wife went to Cologne when her husband was arrested. Apparently Diels, who was still in direct touch with Göring, immediately worked his contacts. Kempner was freed, and in 1936 emigrated first to

Italy and then, in 1939, to America. Only after the end of the war did Kempner and Diels meet again, in Nuremberg.

The former Gestapo chief had first been imprisoned by the British in 1945. Naturally he did all he could to get in touch with Robert Kempner, and finally, as Diels liked to say later in the Witness House, he "had a stroke of luck." On November 1, 1945 the two men sat facing each other in the Nuremberg Palace of Justice, to record a declaration made under oath. In his statement, Diels spoke of his list of planned arrests in 1933 as if he had had nothing at all to do with it. "I myself and my colleagues," claimed Diels, "tried to oppose this wave of terror."

Robert Kempner knew very well that that was only half the truth, for during his time as the head of the Gestapo, Diels had made some extremely dubious decisions about protective custody and the persecution of Jews. Later, tactics of intimidation were based on his decisions. Diels had become unpopular with the SS only when he had tried to oppose unchecked abuses in the many camps set up all over the country during the first few months after the Nazis came to power. The camps were located in former military barracks or Stormtrooper quarters. Diels saw to it that these unauthorized detention centers came under state control. In the process, it is true that many people who had been illegally held were set free—but this was also the beginning of the system of concentration camps.

It would have been wide of the mark, then, to regard the man as an opponent of the Nazi regime, and for that very reason there were several on the prosecution team who considered Rudolf Diels a potential defendant. However, Kempner had something else in mind. The statement drawn up by the U.S. prosecutor that day, November 1, 1945, when he interrogated Diels under oath, hardly uncovered the full truth in the case of the former Gestapo chief, but rather went some way toward exculpating him. In return, very much in the spirit of their old friendship, Kempner required another favor from Diels.

"He had his eye on his career and women," Kempner said of Rudolf Diels in his memoirs. "Above all, he had a certain love of adventure." In Nuremberg, Kempner still seemed to feel some fondness for Diels the gambler and ladies' man. But of course he was not giving either Diels or Hitler's adjutant Wiedemann accommodation at the Witness House out of pure altruism. Kempner needed witnesses who had been as close as possible to the center of Nazi power and could tell the inside story. From Wiedemann, he expected inside knowledge of the close circle around Hitler. Diels, as head of the Gestapo, had seen up close the mysterious Reichstag fire of 1933, a key event in the early period of Nazi rule. He could also provide many details from his intimate knowledge of the defendant Göring. He had known everyone who was anyone.

"We wanted to find out as much as possible as quickly as possible," Kempner told me years later at the Hotel Sonnenhof in Königstein, when I showed him one of the two visitors' books from the Witness House. "That meant talking to certain people with whom one might not otherwise have shared a cup of tea." This was in 1987. The old gentleman, eighty-eight at that time, sat very upright in his armchair. He leafed through the visitors' book with his slightly shaky hands, nodding when a name he knew came up. "Look at that—another of them who couldn't remember anything," he said once, with satisfaction. "But we showed him how to jog his memory."

In November 1945, the prosecutors were still searching feverishly for every single piece of the jigsaw puzzle that could help them in tracing Nazi crimes back to those really responsible wherever possible. It is true that the bureaucrats of death had kept records of just about everything, but at this time some of the crucial papers were not yet accessible. For instance, in the fall of 1945 the prosecutors still knew nothing about the Wannsee Conference of January 1942, when it was decided to implement the "Final Solution." Those records were not found until the spring of 1947. "There were the dead, there were orders," Kempner remembered in his memoirs, but at the time of the main trial there was no survey yet available of the way the Nazi murderers had gone about their work. So Kempner thought it perfectly legitimate to call even heavily incriminated former Nazi functionaries to the witness stand. "Murderers can tell the truth about their murderous colleagues—never mind what their motives for doing so are."

Rudolf Diels himself, in fact, was not inclined to mince words in assessing his benefactor Kempner. Once, when he was talking to the lawyer Kranzbühler at the Witness House, the conversation came around to the U.S. prosecutor and his methods of interrogation. Diels looked at the defense attorney, grinning, and remarked succinctly of his former colleague in Berlin: "A real Gestapo man, he just happened to be racially handicapped."

Kranzbühler presumably met Diels in the hall of the house when the latter was waiting to be taken for a session of questioning. The former Gestapo boss was still in the strict custody of Countess Kálnoky, and could not leave his room. Nor was anyone in the house really supposed to know about his presence. However, Hoffmann had long ago spread the news of this illustrious guest's identity. Gisela Limberger was therefore in the know when she came to the door of the Witness House, not long after the arrival of Diels. Limberger, a lively, not unattractive woman of fifty-two, had been Göring's librarian and private secretary—and she was very well informed about Diels, at least where his love life was concerned.

She talked cheerfully, said the countess in her later account, about Diels's wedding to a member of Göring's family; according to her own account of it, she had been present herself. The woman had loved Diels passionately, Gisela said, and their subsequent divorce had been terrible for her. Kálnoky liked gossip of this kind. When the Countess took Diels's meal up to his room next day, he offered her a place to sit down on a corner of the Krülles' bed. What he told her then, or something like it, he also confirmed at an interrogation by U.S. officers.

His marriage to Ilse Göring in 1938, he said, had been contracted out of "pure fear." The fear, however, was not his own but his future wife's fear for him. Diels described her at Nuremberg as Göring's cousin. (According to other sources, Ilse was Göring's sister.) One day, said Diels, she had come to see him and said, "If you want to save yourself, the only way is to marry me." Soon after that, in this version of events, he was summoned to see Göring, who told him not to imagine that he was under his, Göring's, protection just because he was having an affair with a member of the family. Diels told Göring there was nothing in that story at all. But then, it was alleged, Göring had insisted that Diels must marry his cousin now—"for my own satisfaction."

In his room at the Witness House, Diels left no doubt of the reason why the woman had wanted to marry him: "She was in love with me." Then he cast the countess a disarming glance. "Do you finally believe me now?"

Ingeborg Kálnoky had treated Diels with some reserve at first. She and her family had fled to Budapest from the Gestapo, and she did not like having the first chief of that organization in the house. However, Diels did his best to appear an entertaining charmer when he was with her—and to depict himself as a victim of the National Socialist regime. He described, for instance, how he had been arrested after the July Plot of 1944 against Hitler. A little while after that, proceedings for his divorce had begun, he said. They were initiated by Göring, whose adjutant turned up to see Diels in prison one day to inform him: "The Reich Marshal doesn't want a hanged man in his family."

Later that evening the countess sat on her own bed and thought. All the people who came to stay there professed to have been involved, to a greater or lesser extent, with the Resistance movement. Yet, so far, she had not met a single soul in the Witness House who had really done anything concrete to oppose Hitler.

THE GENERAL WITH THE RED SCARF

The man wore a dark blue beret and a red silk scarf. He was tall and so thin that his uniform tunic with the epaulets cut off hung loose around his shoulders as if it were on a scarecrow. When he took off the beret, he revealed an almost entirely bald head with prominent bones at the temples. The eyes were deep-set in their sockets. A death mask of a face, and yet there was also something intriguingly lively in it, something that involuntarily attracted attention, like a flower in a pile of rubble—it was his mouth, a strikingly beautiful, sensuous mouth.

Countess Kálnoky stood at the window of the Witness House watching the man as he came up to the front door with the other new arrivals. "He kept his distance from the rest of them," she noted later, "and seemed to be deep in thought." Kálnoky instantly had the impression that this man, who, she thought, must be well over fifty, was different from any of the other guests she had so far welcomed to the Witness House. It was November 14, 1945, and a liaison officer had told her to expect four generals and a diplomat that day. The Americans regarded them all as prisoners of war, and they were driven up in two U.S. vehicles with an officer escorting them. The officer was Lieutenant Wulff, a very friendly U.S. soldier who spoke extremely good German. The countess was to see him quite often in future.

The mistress of the house was very uneasy about having to guard POWs as well as playing hostess to the other witnesses, but the lieutenant reassured her. They were gentlemen, he said; there would be an extra guard on duty outside the Witness House, that was all. But the man in the beret, alone among them, also had a personal bodyguard who was to escort him to his room. The countess was astonished—was the man so dangerous that a watch had to be kept on him even in this house? His name was Erwin Lahousen. Kálnoky had never heard of any general of that name—although the other three military men were well-known as top brass in the Wehrmacht.

Ulrich Kessler, who already had a reputation among the Americans for being very laid-back, was regarded as the most prominent of these generals. As a major general in the Luftwaffe, he had last been stationed in Norway, where he had been in command of special operations such as air raids. He wore a monocle when map-reading. As soon as the instrument of surrender was signed, Kessler had tried to get away in a U-boat bound for Argentina. But the U.S. navy intercepted the submarine, and Kessler was taken to America. In his prison camp, the German general had attempted to shake hands with the highest-ranking U.S. officer, as if nothing had happened. The American gave the German the brush-off.

As many other top German military men later would be, Kessler was interrogated for weeks at the Interrogation Center of the American War Department in Fort Hunt, a complex of log cabins in Virginia near Washington, D.C. So were the Hungarian general Kàlmàn Hardy and Emil von Rintelen, a diplomat who had been a special envoy attached to Hitler's Foreign Office. These three men were flown back to Germany just before the beginning of the trial in Nuremberg. When they arrived at the Witness House on November 14, 1945, they were all wearing the same plain U.S. Army shirts, and the countess soon found out that there was a special reason for that. On the flight back to Europe, the little company had stopped off in Paris, where some members of the American prosecution were staying temporarily during the preparation phase for the tribunal. As the three Germans with their cases waited outside the Gare de l'Est to be taken farther, a car with two men in it, presumed to be GIs, suddenly drove up. The men snatched the POWs' baggage and raced away—the cases were never seen again.

The fourth general was Ernst Köstring, an elderly man with an angular face who had been a military attaché in Moscow. He too had come from the camp in Virginia, although a few days earlier than the others. Köstring, like Lahousen, the man with the red silk scarf, had obviously spent some time in the witnesses' wing of the Nuremberg courthouse building before being moved to Novalisstrasse.

The countess showed the new guests their rooms, which were all in the annex building. When she came back to the main house, loud music was playing in the study, and Kálnoky heard Elise Krülle muttering crossly to herself in the kitchen. Obviously Scheidt, the OKW officer, had been listening to another news broadcast, and then, as always, had forgotten to switch the radio off.

Kálnoky was just about to turn it off when a piece by George Frideric Handel was announced. She sank into a chair to listen to the concert, and the music was so pleasant that she soon forgot everything else. Suddenly there was a knock on the door, and the tall general with the red silk scarf asked if he could join her. He had heard the music outside. The countess signed to him to come in, and Lahousen sat down in a corner while his guard hovered near the door.

For several minutes they sat together in the study, both of them lost in their own thoughts, carried away by the music of Handel. But suddenly Kálnoky heard a sob. She looked at Lahousen, and could hardly believe her eyes. The general with his unusual silk scarf was sitting rapt in his chair, his head buried in his hands, weeping bitterly. At first Kálnoky was at a loss. Then she rose to her feet, sat down near him, and laid a hand on his arm. They sat like that for a while as he went on weeping quietly. After a while he raised his head, looked at the countess, and said, "It's the first music I've heard for months, and Handel's 'Largo' too—" Lahousen paused. "I love it so much."

The general spoke with an Austrian accent, the countess noticed, and he was a good deal younger than he looked. Born in Vienna in 1897, he had lived for a long time in Linz, the city where Hitler too had spent his youth. But unlike some of the other guests at the Witness House, men who despite their assurances to the contrary had followed the Führer obediently for years, the forty-eight-year-old Lahousen had done all he could in the past to blow Hitler up. Erwin Lahousen von Vivremont, a member of the minor aristocracy, had been part of the Resistance, and it was a miracle that he was still alive.

General Lahousen had belonged to the circle around Admiral Wilhelm Canaris, who had been head of the Abwehr intelligence department in the Reich War Ministry (1935) and of the department of foreign intelligence in the Wehrmacht High Command (1928). Canaris was executed in April 1945, just before the end of the war. "They hanged him not just once but repeatedly," the countess says Lahousen told her in the Witness House. "In between times they revived him so that he could experience the torture all over again." However, we may doubt whether the general really said anything of the kind to her. He was a taciturn man, and the countess sometimes liked to embroider an incident.

The relationship between Canaris and Lahousen, however, must have been very close, like the bond between a father and a son. Lahousen had been working as an intelligence expert in Vienna when, in 1938, Hitler forcibly annexed Austria during the Anschluss. Later Wilhelm Canaris recruited him for his department at the Wehrmacht High Command in Germany. When the Austrian arrived in the German capital, Colonel Hans Oster showed him the ropes. Oster was one of the most important men in the military Resistance to Hitler, and as Lahousen recollected during the trial, from the first he made no secret of his opinion that there was "a criminal ruling the Reich."

Lahousen became head of Abwehr II, the department responsible for acts of sabotage. A few weeks after the beginning of the war in 1939, at the instigation of Oster, he got hold of the first consignment of explosives for an assassination attempt on Hitler. This attempt had been planned for November 1939, but it fell through because of an attack on Hitler in the Munich Beer Cellar a few days before the chosen date. The bomb made by the Führer's would-be assassin Georg Elser, a trained joiner, went off, but Hitler himself had left the beer cellar ten minutes earlier, and as a result only innocent bystanders were injured.

Almost four years later, in February 1943, Oster asked for Lahousen's help again, this time with ignition devices and explosives that were to be disguised as a present. Lahousen packed a crate with explosives, and his Abwehr colleague Hans von Dohnanyi was to send it on to the Army Group Center headquarters in Smolensk. The plan was to fill two cognac bottles with explosives, making it look like a gift to a friendly officer, and smuggle them into the Führer's aircraft when he visited the Army Group Center headquarters in March 1943. All seemed to be going according to plan: after Hitler's visit the cognac bottles were placed on board his plane, and the aircraft took off. But the baggage hold was too cold, and the explosive failed to ignite while the plane was in the air.

After the July Plot of 1944, Oster, Dohnanyi, and many other Resistance members were executed by the Nazis. Lahousen survived because by this time he had been transferred to the front. And he knew an extraordinary number of details straight from the command center of death. On many occasions, and as an officer from Linz, a city favored by Hitler, he had represented Admiral Canaris at Wehrmacht leadership committees and discussions with the Führer. The Austrian thus not only gained deep insight into the leadership structures of the Nazi regime, but he also knew how individual National Socialists had reacted to certain measures.

Canaris had told Erwin Lahousen to keep a service journal of his experiences. The original was presumably burned after the admiral's arrest, but the Abwehr officer had made copies and attached them to his own departmental service records. This document itself suffered severe damage in an air raid, but using the clues that Lahousen could provide, the Allies were able to find parts of it later.

In May 1945 the British took the Austrian general prisoner and interned him in a camp at Bad Nenndorf. He had been severely wounded in the last months of the war, and his treatment in the camp obviously left something to be desired: Lahousen was going steadily downhill. In the fall of 1945 he was taken to Nuremberg, where he was initially held in the prison attached to the courthouse. On October 22 he sent his wife a telegram from prison, telling her in English, "I am here as a witness, so don't worry." He added that he was "physically fit," but that was certainly a considerable exaggeration. In fact, at the age of forty-eight, he had serious heart trouble, which was probably why he was moved to Novalisstrasse that November.

In the study of the Witness House the music had died away, and the general was in control of himself again. Only now did the countess notice how unkempt he looked. His jacket was greasy, his haggard cheekbones were overgrown with stubble, and his body odor suggested that he could do with a bath. "Can I find anything to help you?" she asked diplomatically. "I have no soap or razor blades," replied Lahousen. Kálnoky soon had an answer to that problem: this was the time to call on the aid of Hoffmann the photographer. She went upstairs and knocked on Hoffmann's door. Reluctantly, Hitler's old acquaintance produced a piece of soap and some razor blades out of his reserves of items from U.S. stores, and she passed them on to the former Resistance man.

At supper Lahousen already looked a good deal better. Hoffmann immediately embarked on a conversation with General Köstring, who had once been a military attaché to the German embassy in Moscow. The photographer had once met him at a reception there. "Don't you remember? I came with Ribbentrop," he told the general. Then he explained that Hitler had asked him to accompany the foreign minister when he was going to Russia to conclude the nonaggression pact. "I was to tell Hitler about my impression of Stalin," claimed Hoffmann, speculating that the Führer had a poor opinion of his diplomats' powers of judgment. The countess noticed both Köstring and Ambassador Rintelen, a tall Westphalian in his mid-forties, stiffen at these words. However, the discussion soon turned to other subjects. Now General Kessler was sounding off about the Luftwaffe and the conduct of the war. "We only had to win the war first," someone in the company around the table put it. "Then we'd have dealt with Hitler and the Party in short order."

The discussion went on late into the night. Lahousen took very little part in it. He was noticeably reserved for the next few days as well. Meanwhile, the generals did not seem to take much interest in their Austrian colleague—indeed, the countess had the impression that they were avoiding him. At this point no one in the Witness House knew that Lahousen was going to be a crucial witness for the prosecution. His reserved manner, however, was striking in that company. Lahousen's nature was far from jovial anyway; he cracked no jokes, he told neither anecdotes nor heroic wartime stories, and indeed he obviously saw nothing glorious about the recent past, as the other guests were surprised and displeased to observe.

In the Witness House, you were soon hardly even aware that the generals were prisoners of war, although none of them could leave the property. The diplomat Rintelen, in fact, complained that he was the only government official staying in Novalisstrasse to be "held prisoner against the tenets of international law." Apart from that, however, the gentlemen clearly enjoyed the young countess's charm and hospitality. They had settled into the little place very comfortably, and would each take a constitutional in the garden after lunch. One after another they marched around the house, climbed past what remained of the walls of the ruined garage, and so made their rounds.

Gerhard Krülle, who was often out and about locally, sometimes watched this spectacle surreptitiously from a distance. The sight of these famous generals, grandees of the Nazi Reich, goose-stepping around his parents' house struck him as unintentionally comic. It passed through Gerhard's mind that his father would never come to terms with it. But then he also thought his father probably wouldn't have survived the war mentally unharmed, as he later told me.

Ernst Köstring, the eldest of the military men and a cavalry general, even went jogging every day, taking paths that could be seen from the house. Aged sixty-nine, he would jog for half an hour whatever the weather. Elise Krülle had a simple explanation for the old gentleman's ostentatious athleticism. In spite of his age, so gossip went in the kitchen, the general had recently fathered a child—so of course he had to keep fit.

But Erwin Lahousen was the only guest who went for interrogation at the courthouse building almost every day. Usually it was a young U.S. soldier called Richard Sonnenfeldt who came to collect him. Sonnenfeldt was a very intelligent young man with dark hair and a cheerful nature. He was only twenty-two, but he was considered one of the best interpreters on the prosecution, and he had forged a personal link with Erwin Lahousen. At first the Austrian general had been reserved. He was deeply insulted by the poor treatment he had received in the British POW camp, and at the same time he felt vaguely guilty. Almost all his colleagues from the legendary Abwehr department had been killed by the Nazis, but he had survived. Why? What kind of value would there be in his statement now?

Sonnenfeldt was the absolute opposite of the melancholy general, yet he too might well have felt bitter, for as a young Jew he had survived the war and the Nazi period when millions of his coreligionists were murdered. Sonnenfeldt had been born in Gardelegen, near Magdeburg, in 1938. In 1938 his parents sent him and his younger brother to boarding school in England to keep the boys safe from the Nazis. For the first few years, all was well. Then Germany and Britain declared war on each other, and because Sonnenfeldt was over fifteen he was interned. As a German citizen, like many other Jews who had fled from their native land, he was placed in a camp along with Nazi activists.

With courage, chutzpah, and a great deal of luck, however, he later managed to diverge from his apparently predestined path. Embarking on adventurous sea voyages, he reached first Australia, later Bombay, and then, on his own initiative, set off for the United States. Sonnenfeldt returned to Germany as a U.S. soldier. Before coming to Nuremberg in the summer of 1945, he had visited the recently liberated concentration camp at Dachau. The piles of corpses, he wrote later in his memoirs, did not shock him as much as the sight of the survivors. The young man had tried to talk to people in Dachau, but faced with their immeasurable grief he could only stammer a few words.

Why had he been spared? Was it chance or providence? The young soldier could not get these questions out of his mind. Lahousen was probably asking himself something similar. Reading between the lines of his interrogation records, we can tell what kind of answer Lahousen found. Just because he, almost alone of his Abwehr group, had survived, the Austrian officer now had a kind of higher duty to "bear witness" to what had happened, as Lahousen himself put it. So he began to cooperate with the Americans.

It was Richard Sonnenfeldt's job to keep an eye on several special guests at the Witness House. As he had no fear of making new friends, he got into conversations with many of those guests. Decades later, the former ambassador Rintelen remembered the young man. He mentioned him, as Private Sonnenfeldt, in a handwritten letter to the countess. That made me decide to try finding Sonnenfeldt myself.

"The Witness House? Yes, of course I remember it," the old gentleman shouted down the telephone at me. It was spring 2005, and I had finally tracked him down at his Long Island home. By now Sonnenfeldt was eighty-two, rather hard of hearing, and not as active as he used to be, so he told me, after suffering a stroke. But his memory was evidently perfectly intact.

"Lahousen and Diels, ah yes, those two were key witnesses at the trial," he told me in his deep voice. "I often spoke to them."

Of the U.S. soldiers on the prosecution who used to go in and out of the Witness House, Richard Sonnenfeldt was one of the very few still alive in the first decade of the present century, when I interviewed him. His superior officers of the time were all long dead. He once got into trouble with them over Lahousen. One evening, the young U.S. soldier was to take the general for an interrogation by Colonel John Harlan Amen, a high-ranking member of the section of the American prosecution that was particularly concerned with Wehrmacht personnel. Meanwhile a new guest had arrived at the Witness House, one whom Lahousen probably knew from the past: Paul Leverkühn, a rather enigmatic figure. Leverkühn, a lawyer, had worked in Istanbul for Canaris and the Abwehr; later, after the founding of the Federal Republic of Germany, he was to be a Christian Democratic deputy in the Bundestag. He was now appearing at Nuremberg in his legal capacity, although no one knew which of the defendants he was representing.

Leverkühn had a very good relationship with General William J. Donovan, a prominent figure among the American prosecutors, and it may have been because of this relationship that he was accommodated at the Witness House. The two men probably knew each other from their secret service assignments, for Donovan, nicknamed Wild Bill, was the founder and head of the American OSS (Office of Strategic Services), the predecessor of the CIA. Speaking for Donovan, Leverkühn invited Erwin Lahousen to a dinner with the U.S. general that November evening in 1945, assuring him that his appointment with Sonnenfeldt and Amen could wait. Lahousen went to the dinner, but did not see much of Donovan, who arrived late. Amen complained to Lahousen the next morning, asking indignantly what he had thought he was doing missing their appointment. The Austrian, as Sonnenfeldt remembered later, made a helpless gesture. He had been told to get into Donovan's car, he said—"I'm only a prisoner of war, what was I supposed to do?"

This incident took place on November 22, 1945, two days after the beginning of the main trial, and thus at a time when tension was at its height for the prosecutors. The affair made such waves that Donovan took offense. Shortly thereafter he left the American team headed by the chief prosecutor, Robert Jackson. Leverkühn left the Witness House a few days after this fateful dinner. Sonnenfeldt was reprimanded for not preventing Lahousen's excursion, and even the countess felt distressed, wondering whether this stupid incident couldn't have been avoided.

Ingeborg Kálnoky lived in constant fear of doing something wrong in the Witness House. Since the arrival of the generals, she had more frequent contact with members of the American secret service, the CIC. Its agents came to the house to question her as well, which she found very uncomfortable, as she said later.

There was much coming and going of various guests at the villa by now. Luise Jodl, the wife of the Wehrmacht general who was one of the defendants, stayed there several times when she came to Nuremberg to talk to her husband's attorneys, Jahreiss and Exner. The two defense lawyers had stayed briefly at the Witness House themselves, but they were soon given quarters elsewhere. Frau Jodl had married her husband only a few months before the end of the war, and now she was moving heaven and earth to help him. Many people admired her self-sacrificing devotion. She arrived in Nuremberg just before the beginning of the trial, walking all the way from Berchtesgaden. Father Flynn, who was always very well informed about what went on in and around the courthouse, said that Frau Jodl had tried to hand in "two eggs and an orange" for her husband at the prison gates. Countess Kálnoky, who did not like this lady much herself, said that Luise Jodl gave her the impression of being like "an animal at bay."

The company at the Witness House was a motley assortment. Alongside the generals, who seemed more at a loss for ways to occupy themselves every day, a high-ranking National Socialist official had moved into the house. His name was Bertus Gerdes. He was a blond and blue-eyed man who looked as if he had sprung from one of the Nazi Lebensborn* institutions. His statement at the trial was intended to incriminate the defendant Ernst Kaltenbrunner severely at a later stage. Kaltenbrunner had once been Heinrich Himmler's right-hand man, and from 1943 was head of the Reich Security Central Office (RSHA), which oversaw the Gestapo. Göring's secretary Gisela Limberger commented on the subject of Diels and other former favorites of her boss. Two former mistresses of Ernst Kaltenbrunner were also said to have stayed at the Witness House now and then, as Sonnenfeldt remembered. "We tried to get something out of them." However, there is no evidence other than this remark of their presence as guests in Novalisstrasse.

Many of the men and women staying there had to share a room with another guest, which did not contribute much to a relaxed atmosphere. And then there was the countess's baby, Bobbie, as the little girl was soon called. She usually lay in a little wicker baby basket on the kitchen table. She cried a lot, as the countess remembered even many years later—and Cuci the nursemaid left her to cry.

* The Lebensborn ("spring of life") program consisted of several homes designed to bring up blond, blue-eyed children as part of the master race. Many of them later discovered, as adults, that their unknown fathers had been members of the SS.

With so much coming and going, Ingeborg Kálnoky was bound to feel insecure and sometimes overtaxed. So it may well have been pleasant for her that Father Flynn looked in at Novalisstrasse with conspicuous regularity. Generally the priest brought something useful with him: instant coffee, for example. There always seemed to be a shortage of coffee, in spite of the generous rations supplied by the U.S. army.

On such occasions Elise Krülle would make a pot of coffee while Father Flynn and the countess sat in the study. The priest listened patiently when Ingeborg Kálnoky told him at length about her daily needs and anxieties, and he was usually able to offer good advice. So the countess could overlook the fact that Flynn seemed more and more attracted to her, and not only in the realm of domestic attention.

However, Elise Krülle, that shrewd woman, soon guessed that the priest harbored some very worldly feelings. Her son Gerhard also followed Fabian Flynn's visits with close interest, and it struck the boy too that the priest was greatly taken by the lady of the house.

TRENCH WARFARE AND
A FOUNTAIN PEN

General Köstring's fountain pen had gone missing. A pen like that was a treasure in those days, when hardly anyone owned so much as a watch, so the officer did not find his loss at all amusing. Köstring asked guest after guest if anyone had seen his pen, always pointing to the study table. That was where he had left it, he said. Ambassador Rintelen, who was sitting reading in an armchair as usual, cast the general a look of disapproval. "Is all this so important that you have to keep telling everyone about it?" he snapped at the general.

Köstring looked at the diplomat for a moment, speechless, and then suddenly exploded. "It's all very well for you to talk," he told the former ambassador angrily. "You were able to put on airs as a civilian during the war while we soldiers were risking our lives." Rintelen looked up from his book, and was quick with his retort. "You generals, you mean? When did anyone ever see a general at the front?" he inquired sharply. "But I suppose that as military attaché in Moscow you felt really close to the front line, didn't you, General?"

At this moment the countess entered the room, and with her most winning smile came between the combatants. "Oh, gentlemen, why don't we talk about something more amusing?" Feeling embarrassed, old Köstring immediately apologized for his outburst of bad manners, and Rintelen muttered that all this waiting about made him feel very unwell. When the countess was going to her chair at the table, she suddenly felt a hard object of some kind underfoot—there lay the fountain pen.

Since the opening of the tribunal on November 20, 1945, the atmosphere in the Witness House had been increasingly edgy. Some of the guests were prey to vague anxieties; others obviously felt worse by the day, for now that the trial was beginning, matters suddenly seemed to be really serious. But while Lahousen was still taken away every day for interrogation, no one seemed interested in the other guests anymore. Presumably that was even more intolerable than daily questioning. However, Lahousen himself seemed increasingly nervous. At this point, the prosecutors were still presenting their indictments during the public sessions in court. The Austrian was soon to feature as their first witness, and no doubt he felt the responsibility weighing heavily on him. Sometimes the countess found him biting his nails as he listened to the radio. A general who shed tears and bit his nails: Lahousen did not exactly fit her ideal of the opposite sex, although in peacetime he had surely been an attractive man.

The Americans also seemed concerned with Erwin Lahousen's state of mind, and one day they sent an unusual visitor to the Witness House. The girl was dark-haired and rather on the plump side, thought the countess, who herself was slender and willowy. "This is a good friend of the general's, she's going to stay with him for three days," explained the U.S. soldier escorting her, but her visit, he added, had to be kept "strictly confidential." Sure enough, the girl stayed three nights with Lahousen while his guard, who usually slept in the room with him, took up a position outside the door. Whether Lahousen really knew the young woman, and how this visit came to be allowed, even Richard Sonnenfeldt could not say in retrospect. "I expect one of us asked him what gave him pleasure," surmised the old man sixty years later. The countess noted dryly in her own account that "the court could prescribe special medicine for special witnesses."

As the day when Lahousen was to give evidence drew closer, the countess decided that the general could not appear in court in his shabby jacket. She went down to Elise Krülle's room in the cellar, and asked first if there was any news of her missing husband. No, Elise had heard nothing since a letter from him that had arrived in September, in which he wrote that everything was all right, and he still thought it would all end well. However, the letter had been postmarked as long ago as April 1945, and Elise thought that showed there was no point in hoping for her husband's return now.

There was someone who urgently needed a suit to wear, said the countess, finally coming to the point. Thereupon the helpful Elise looked through her wardrobe, and soon she found a dark men's suit still in quite reasonable shape. The sleeves and the legs were short for a man of Lahousen's height, but they could be let down a little. Finally Elise Krülle ironed her husband's good suit and the countess took it to Lahousen. The general was both embarrassed and pleased, as she said later.

The next morning Lahousen was sitting in the study early. Kálnoky thought he looked very well groomed, so when she heard a radio report of the Abwehr officer's appearance in court that evening she was rather annoyed. The reporter, a man by the name of Gaston Oulmann, said that Lahousen had been dressed "more like a post office clerk than a general."

But Erwin Lahousen's evidence at the tribunal was sensational. He unsparingly described the criminal methods that

Hitler had used in preparing for war, and the fact that the top brass of the Wehrmacht knew about them and were themselves involved in these dirty tricks. During his testimony, the general had been allowed to sit rather than stand, as was customary, because of his heart problems. Speaking in a calm and very matter-of-fact voice, he began going into detail. Directly before the Polish campaign of late summer 1939, the Abwehr had been given a mysterious assignment: they were to have ready Polish uniforms and items of equipment—field books and similar Polish accessories—in preparation for something entitled Operation Himmler.

An SS man turned up one day to collect these things. The Abwehr officers were able to work out what they were for a little later, from an internal Wehrmacht report. A number of concentration camp inmates, disguised in Polish uniforms, had been forced to attack the German radio station in the Silesian town of Gleiwitz. As "evidence" of the alleged Polish attack, the SS had left a dead concentration camp prisoner at the scene. Early in the morning the next day—September 1, 1939—German troops invaded Poland. German propaganda presented this move as a blow struck in self-defense: "Last night Polish regular soldiers also fired on our own troops for the first time," declared Hitler a little later in the Reichstag.

Operation Himmler had been so secret that even the trained intelligence agents of Canaris's own department could not find out much more about it. To this day, not all the details of the operation have been cleared up: for instance, the question of who exactly wore the Polish uniforms, or indeed if they were used at all. But Lahousen for one had heard later that all who took part in the operation—not just the concentration camp inmates disguised as Poles, but even the SS men involved—had then been killed to eliminate accessories to the fact and potential informers about this faked pretext for war. That was not, as it turned out, the whole truth, for the leader of the operation, SS Sturmbannführer Alfred Naujocks, survived, and he talked about it later.

Soon after this cleverly staged excuse for the outbreak of war, there were several other discussions in the "Führer train," as the vehicle in which Hitler traveled was called. Lahousen also knew all about that. He had accompanied the head of the Abwehr, Canaris, to the meetings, in which then foreign minister Ribbentrop, Keitel as the head of the OKW, and Jodl in his capacity at the time as head of the Wehrmacht General Staff, had all taken part, with Hitler himself putting in an appearance now and then. "Do you recognize Ribbentrop here in the court?" Colonel Amen, who was questioning him, now asked. Lahousen turned to look at the defendants' bench and said calmly, "I do." He identified Ribbentrop as the man in the front row, third from the left.

The discussions on board the train were about the planned bombing of Warsaw. There was also talk of a project that Keitel, as Lahousen now recollected verbatim, had called "political reallocation." Alluding to a phrase of Hitler's creation, it entailed the shooting en masse of Polish intellectuals, aristocrats, clerics, and of course Jews. Canaris had vigorously opposed these plans, said Lahousen now in court, and he quoted his mentor: "One day the world will hold the Wehrmacht, before whose eyes these things happened, jointly responsible for such methods." Keitel, however, had merely replied that everything had "already been decided by the Führer."

Another operation was discussed at a meeting in the Führer train. The Abwehr, Ribbentrop decreed, was to stage a revolt in the Galician part of Ukraine, sending as many Polish farms as possible up in flames and killing the local Jews. Again and again, Lahousen told the court, words like "liquidate" or "eliminate" had been used in this discussion—used, indeed, by the defendants now present in the courtroom.

Wearing large headphones, Lahousen sat in his chair on the witness stand and added detail after detail. What he said was deadly, particularly for Keitel, Jodl, and Ribbentrop. The Austrian officer described various meetings with those men, and he also remembered orders that Keitel had given over the phone. The OKW head, known as "Lakeitel"* in Wehrmacht circles because he was so subservient to Hitler, had ordered him, Lahousen, to organize the murder of a prominent French army officer whom Keitel wanted out of the way. According to Lahousen's account, a second French general was also to be assassinated. The Abwehr officer went on to describe how the planned mass murder of Russian prisoners of war had been put into effect by SS commandos with the express approval of the top brass of the Wehrmacht. He did not omit to mention that groups of British prisoners were also ordered to be shot.

Toward the end of Lahousen's examination, the prosecuting attorney Harlan Amen drew the attention of the court to a box that he had deposited in the courtroom. It contained the remains of Lahousen's service journal, and resembled a precious relic that no one was to touch. An incendiary bomb had left the paper of the original so brittle that it would have crumbled at a touch if taken out, and it was already badly frayed around the edges, with dark burn marks on the text here and there. The Americans had very carefully had a copy of this valuable document made; not even Lahousen himself was allowed to read his old journal in the original.

---

* German *Lackei* = lackey; Keitel becomes "lackey Keitel" in this coinage.

When the court rose at lunchtime, the prison psychologist Gustave M. Gilbert asked some of the defendants for their response to Lahousen's evidence. "That traitor!" said Göring angrily. "There's one we forgot on July 20." Jodl too saw Lahousen's evidence as treachery, although in another sense. If it had been Lahousen's opinion that they were treading the wrong path, he ought to have said so there and then "instead of betraying his honor as an officer," complained the former Wehrmacht chief of staff. When Gilbert shared these and other such remarks with Lahousen later, Lahousen just commented bitterly, "They speak of honor now that millions have been murdered." He had felt in duty bound, Lahousen went on, to say all these things. "I have to speak for those they murdered; I'm the only one left."

Lahousen had retrieved his honor in the courtroom, and he returned to the Witness House a different man. When the countess asked how he was feeling, he just said, as she remembered later, that it had all gone "perfectly naturally, as a matter of course." He added, "I would never have thought I could be so calm and composed." Later, when the evening news came over the radio, it was almost impossible to hear the account of his evidence because everyone in the villa was talking. Many of the guests were probably not very keen to know exactly what Lahousen had said about the Wehrmacht. Lahousen himself took just as little interest in the anxieties and concerns of the agitated company in the Witness House.

When the defense cross-examined Lahousen the next morning, his answers showed a perceptible new self-confidence. Otto Nelte, Keitel's defense counsel, tried to put all kinds of phrases into the officer's mouth so that he could retrieve a little credit for his client. Hadn't Keitel said, again and again, that officers with problems of conscience could turn to him in confidence?

"No," replied Lahousen, "I certainly had no such impression." Hadn't the OKW chief called only for military, not political, obedience? No, said Lahousen again, Keitel had definitely wanted a "National Socialist Wehrmacht," and he would never have tolerated any officer around him who did not give "unconditional obedience to the Führer."

Lahousen had fought his battle in the courtroom, but now an unfocused form of trench warfare began in the Witness House. The newspaper reports of what the Austrian officer had said on the witness stand must have come as something of a shock to many of the other guests. Over the following days, the talk at mealtimes kept turning to questions of loyalty, doing one's duty, keeping one's oath. What exactly was said we do not know. All that Countess Kálnoky would say about it, many years later, was that the "setup" of the trial had been heavily criticized. An old lady then, she told me in her pleasant voice with its husky Thuringian tinge that "the victors were sitting in judgment on individual representatives of the country that had lost the war. And a good many of the guests in my house didn't like that."

She was talking to me in her little apartment in Cleveland, in the middle of the 1990s. Huge snowflakes were falling outside, and soon the streets were impassable. Inside, the TV set was on. Meanwhile the old lady sat in a comfortable chair, bringing those memorable days in the Witness House back to life in her stories. There had been snow falling in Nuremberg back then, she remembered. "The guards posted outside had lit themselves a fire in the street because it was so cold," said the countess. "We could see the firelight inside the house." She still vividly remembered the company assembled in the study. "Look, there's Köstring." The old lady pointed to a slightly crumpled photograph, and added, "Hoffmann took that picture." Next to Köstring, another rather blurred face could be made out. "Bertus Gerdes," croaked Kálnoky. "He'd been *Gau** chief of staff in Munich."

Then she took a yellowed newspaper cutting out of a box. It was a photo of a man with a broad face. "Look, that's General Kessler." It was obvious that the generals in particular could not have liked what Lahousen said. Hadn't it been hard enough, they must have thought indignantly, for men in leading positions in the Wehrmacht to do their duty in spite of their reservations about Hitler? Hadn't they taken an oath pledging obedience? And wasn't there always a pressing duty to obey the orders of their superior officers? The gentlemen staying at the Witness House in the winter of 1945 brought up these and other such questions. Erwin Lahousen listened to their discussion for some time without saying a word. Then he suddenly spoke up. "I understand," he said, his voice almost expressionless. "Yesterday's witnesses will probably be tomorrow's defendants."

For a moment all was perfectly quiet in the study. However, the countess soon managed to steer the conversation into calmer waters. She had the gift of switching with perfect ease from profound discussion to the lightest of small talk, usually with the aid of one of her anecdotes. They were only half true, but she could tell them in a way that entertained everyone.

On one of those December evenings in 1945 she aroused particular merriment. Once again new guests had arrived, including Hans Luther, a former Reich chancellor in the days of the Weimar Republic, who had been ambassador to Washington from 1933 to 1937 under the Nazi regime, and Niklas Horthy, son of the Hungarian head of state Miklós Horthy,

---

* *Gau*, meaning "region," was used for administrative regional areas under the Nazis. Each was headed by a Gauleiter.

who had made a pact with Hitler and was now in the witnesses' wing of the jail attached to the Nuremberg courthouse.

The story that Kálnoky told to amuse the company that December evening in 1945 ran something like this: a cousin of hers had lost the tip of his nose while fencing in a dueling fraternity. Don't worry, said the doctor, we'll just stitch it back on again. Unfortunately, she added, her cousin's dog had run off with the tip of his nose, so all the doctor could do was stitch a piece of chicken on the nose instead. The graft worked very well, but after a while it began growing feathers, and from then on her cousin always had to shave his nose.

There was hearty laughter in the study, so the countess said later. Horthy in particular seemed mightily amused. The charming Hungarian kept taking Kálnoky's hand and covering it with kisses. Just then the countess's elder daughter came into the room. Eleonora, a very pretty girl with thick blond braids, probably couldn't sleep. When the ten-year-old saw her mother being so familiar with young Horthy, she stopped dead as if rooted to the spot. Countess Kálnoky explained, repeating the anecdote. Everyone politely laughed again except for little Eleonora, who didn't think the story was at all funny. "But that's not true!" cried the little girl defiantly.

Kálnoky knew dozens of such stories. Presumably people used to tell them by the fireside on long winter evenings in those lonely castles in the country where the countess had once lived. Many of the guests in the Witness House enjoyed her anecdotes as a form of harmless diversion; some may have found such entertainment rather too superficial. Kálnoky's children did not have an entirely easy time with their eloquent mother. Generally they played in the garden, or sat with the nursemaid Cuci in the room where they and Cuci slept, on the first floor a little way from the other bedrooms.

The children were not sent to school, but the countess had quickly found a governess to teach them English. This was Frau Gerschwitz, a middle-aged lady whose unique body odor Kálnoky's son Fárkas could still describe decades later: "Like damp dishcloths."

Countess Kálnoky liked to be the center of attention in any company, and as a very good-looking woman she was used to having all eyes drawn to her. "They admired me, they indulged me," the old lady told me, not without pride, in her little apartment in Cleveland, while the snowflakes went on falling outside. Suddenly a smile came to her painted lips, her eyes twinkled, and an attractively youthful look came into her face, as if it were in soft focus. "And some of them paid court to me," the eighty-seven-year-old added, rather more quietly.

One of those was Scheidt of the OKW. He pursued the countess more and more persistently as time went on, even telling her once that his wife wanted to get divorced. Kálnoky, however, did not feel in the least attracted to the army officer. As we can see from a drawing Hoffmann did of him, he had rather a corpulent figure. She thought him "starchy and sarcastic," not at all the sort of man who appealed to her. She liked lively, entertaining characters; gravity could easily lead to gloom, the down-to-earth could be boring—and nothing was worse than boredom.

The former Gestapo chief Diels, still under house arrest, was another who was always flirting with the lady of the house. Gerhard Krülle, who used to eavesdrop when something interesting seemed to be going on between the guests at the Witness House, found out that he called her his "Maize Countess."* The countess herself was wary of Diels. He could easily have

---

* Presumably alluding to the color of her blond hair.

been a pirate captain, she thought. Hoffmann had already worked out his own theory of why Diels had been sent to Novalisstrasse under house arrest: "The Yanks know he'd never run away from a lady," he said in a large party of people, to general amusement. "Or if he did, it would only be because he was running away *with* her."

The room where Diels was staying was right beside the countess's own bedroom, which was smaller, but had a door out to the same balcony. Besides his weakness for beautiful women, he had another hobbyhorse, botany. He sometimes asked Kálnoky to bring him small plants or seeds from the garden or the nearby wood. Later, in the spring of 1946, she saw that he was growing small mosses, watering them lovingly from the jug of water he kept in his room for washing.

In December 1945 Diels was allowed to leave his room in the Witness House for a while. He had gained permission from the Americans to be under house arrest in a rather more fashionable place, Count Faber-Castell's hunting lodge in Dürrenhembach near Feucht, to the south of Nuremberg. Diels was on friendly terms with the lady of the house, Katharina von Faber-Castell, who had a family connection with the prosecution team: she was a distant cousin of Captain Drexel Sprecher, a colleague of Robert Jackson, the American chief prosecutor. The hunting lodge was a very exclusive place, and a vantage point from which to view the trial at only one remove. Prosecutors, attorneys, and their illustrious witnesses, people like Diels, went there on weekends to discuss matters that could not be brought up at the trial itself, or to hunt deer in the extensive woods.

The Faber-Castell family's castle west of Nuremberg, in Stein, which was also the headquarters of their famous pencil manufacturing company, had been commandeered by the Americans for use by the press corps. Over 250 journalists who had come for the opening of the trial were staying there. They ate in magnificent banquet halls and slept in large group dormitories. Brushing your teeth in the shared bathroom, you might encounter such famous writers as John Steinbeck, Ernest Hemingway, and John Dos Passos, as George W. Herald, correspondent of the American news agency International News Service, later remembered. With the start of the tribunal, Nuremberg had become one of the most interesting places in Europe overnight.

All of a sudden there was vibrant American social life in the ruined city—no one had known much about the place before, apart from pencils, gingerbread, and the marching at the Reich Nazi Party rallies. The new style was especially evident in the Grand Hotel, which had been refurbished in rough and ready fashion, but had hardly had time "to switch from one kind of occupation to another," as Philipp Fehl, one of the American prosecuting team, put it in a delightful essay. Meals at the Grand Hotel—also described in the old days as the "Reich Party Rally Hotel"—were served with the hotel's silver cutlery, still engraved with the eagle and the swastika. There were three bars on the first floor of the hotel, one of them in the Marble Room, which soon became legendary for its constantly changing succession of entertainers. The hotel entrance was guarded by military police, and outside the building, Philipp Fehl saw "cripples and children" waiting to rush to pick up cigarette ends that the more privileged had thrown away.

Inside, there could be trouble. Drexel Sprecher, of the prosecution, once knocked down a U.S. officer who had seized a colleague by the tie. "I felt absolutely in the right of it," Sprecher told me when I visited him in Washington, D.C. "To be on the safe side, however, I left the bar immediately after the incident that evening."

Tickets to the shows in the Marble Room were in great demand. German girls could enter only on the arm of a U.S. soldier. Social life was even more elegant in the Dürrenhembach hunting lodge, to which only handpicked guests were invited. Some of the visitors to the Witness House would have given much to be among the company at the Faber-Castells' house. Gisela Limberger, Göring's secretary, left no stone unturned in her efforts to persuade Diels to get her an invitation to Dürrenhembach. But all he did about it was to send the countess a handwritten note saying that he was having "a very quiet, refreshing time" with the Faber-Castells, and was going to extend his stay in the country a little longer. In the same letter he sent warm wishes to "Fräulein Limberger," although he added that he could not easily fix it for her to "move here for a few days."

So Gisela Limberger had to content herself with the company of an old acquaintance at the Witness House, from whom she had most recently heard when he was still in an Austrian internment camp under interrogation: Hitler's photographer Heinrich Hoffmann.

BIRTHDAY CHECKS FROM THE CIGARETTE KING

Gisela Limberger was one of those guests at the Witness House whose whole world must have collapsed in the preceding months. She had worshiped Hermann Göring like a god. Now she found out from the U.S. officers interrogating her that he had been a war criminal and an art thief—and she had even helped him with his underhanded machinations, although presumably without knowing the whole situation.

When Göring's former private secretary came to Novalisstrasse in November 1945, she had already undergone months of questioning. Limberger was one of a group of sixteen people from whom the Americans hoped to find out more about Göring's financial circumstances and exactly how he had gone about acquiring his works of art. The "last great Renaissance man," as one of his colleagues called him, had assembled an incomparable treasury of masterpieces in his ostentatious country house, Carinhall, on the western outskirts of the Schorfheide forest north of Berlin. Works by Cranach, Rubens, and Rembrandt hung on the walls of the villa. Limberger had at times been responsible for the care of this art collection. She had also kept Göring's accounts and managed his private correspondence, classified his books, and drawn up inventories of paintings and sculptures.

She had met the man who was to be Reich Marshal back in 1930, when Göring was looking for a secretary. Gisela Limberger, aged thirty-seven at the time and unmarried, declined his offer of the position with thanks and decided to train as a librarian. In 1933 Göring, now minister president of Prussia, approached her again. This time he needed someone to sort out his books. Limberger, who was capable, well educated, and honest, did the job to his great satisfaction, but she stayed on at the state library. A year later the Nazi politician once again asked the librarian for her secretarial help, and this time Limberger agreed. Meanwhile, so she told the Americans in Nuremberg, considerable pressure had been put on the staff of the state library to join the National Socialist Party—so she had decided that she would rather walk straight into the lion's den. No one asked about Party membership in Göring's office, she said. On the contrary, Paul Körner, who was Göring's state secretary and a high-up SS functionary, had told her, "It doesn't matter for you girls."

It was a fact that Gisela Limberger had never joined the Nazi Party. "The circles I moved in didn't include Party members," she said under interrogation. Through her sister, who was head of a Berlin hospital and later emigrated, the librarian had contacts with Jewish doctors. One of them was arrested in 1938. "I went to Göring and put in a good word for him," Limberger told the officers interrogating her, and soon after that the man was freed.

Little as Gisela Limberger said she had had to do with Nazi officials, her view of her boss was entirely uncritical. Hundreds of thousands of Reichsmarks passed through her hands on his behalf, she managed millions in his bank account, and she cataloged artworks of incalculable value. In many cases, these were really stolen goods. She was always under great pressure at work on Göring's birthday, when she had to keep a record of the donors of countless presents. When they came to visit, captains of industry like Friedrich Flick and Wilhelm Tengelmann regularly brought valuable gifts, such as paintings, carpets, or sculptures. The "cigarette king," tobacco tycoon Philipp Reemtsma, always gave large sums of money, amounting over time to at least eleven million Reichsmarks, as he himself admitted later.

After the birthday festivities, Göring would put his hand in his pocket, as Gisela Limberger phrased it, bring out the checks he had been given, and tell his secretary to take them to the bank. Around 250,000 Reichsmarks could arrive on just one of his birthdays—although that was not a particularly large amount from the point of view of his secretary, who was used to juggling larger sums. Göring's personal annual salary, she recollected later, was between 200 and 250 million Reichsmarks—and that, she added, did not include the sums he spent on buildings and their maintenance. Limberger had never stopped to wonder where all the money came from, far exceeding a normal governmental salary as it did. She herself received only a modest salary from the Prussian state government, on the civil service scale. Receiving anything extra from her boss had "not been usual," she told one of the U.S. soldiers questioning her.

Göring's private secretary remained unquestioningly loyal to her boss. In April 1945 Göring asked her to come to Berchtesgaden, bringing money and books. The secretary packed a case full of books and left Berlin on one of the last trains out of the city. A day and a half later, on April 23, she tried to make contact with Göring, in vain. He had sent his works of art south in a convoy, and then had his beloved house Carinhall blown up. Soon after that he had gone, with a large number

of hangers-on, to his villa on the Obersalzberg near Berchtesgaden. From there, on that same April 23, 1945, he had sent
a telegram to Berlin declaring himself ready to succeed the
Führer. Göring, thinking that Hitler was already finished, had
miscalculated. Hitler regarded the Reich Marshal's telegram as
high treason and had him arrested. SS men also caught up with
Göring's secretary. They confiscated the case of books and the
cash, and advised her to get out as quickly as possible.

Gisela Limberger, who was the same age as Göring's wife,
Emmy, had always been in close contact with her boss's family, so she then went to Göring's sister in Mattsee, Austria. The
Allies found the librarian there in May 1945. She was taken
to Altaussee in Austria, where a special U.S. army unit had set
up a team to look into the Nazis' art thefts. Göring's private
secretary and various other members of his staff were interrogated for weeks on end, and as a result of their research the
investigators drew up a list of over twenty thousand valuable
items, including paintings, tapestries, and porcelain. Göring
had accumulated two thousand items for himself personally;
others were destined for the "Führer Museum" that was to be
founded in Linz.

Heinrich Hoffmann had been involved in this enterprise as
artistic adviser, and consequently in the summer of 1945 the
Americans also questioned the photographer of so many Third
Reich dignitaries—although not in Altaussee, but in Stadelheim Prison in Munich. Hoffmann too had accumulated an
impressive gallery of paintings. He collected pictures of the
Romantic period, including several magnificent works. Now
he was having some difficulty in explaining to the Americans
how he had come by these paintings. "If I can't give you a very
clear account, that's because thousands of pictures have passed
through my hands," Hoffmann apologized. Life was hard,

even for Hitler's photographer. "I didn't take any pleasure in my pictures in the end," Hoffmann complained in his interrogation, "because I was almost always away."

Hoffmann's statements about the art thefts had presumably not revealed much to the Americans. Gisela Limberger, however, obviously had valuable information to provide, so she was taken to Nuremberg to give evidence against Göring at the trial if necessary. It never came to that, and she must have been relieved. In spite of all the unpleasant revelations about her former boss's criminal obsession with art, she still felt very close to his family, and later she was to remain in touch for a long time with Göring's widow, Emmy.

There was practically nothing for Gisela Limberger to do now in the Witness House, and so she followed the evening discussions with great interest. It was on such evenings that Bertus Gerdes told his shocking story. Until recently this tall, fair-haired man had been a fervent Nazi and Gau chief of staff in Munich, meaning that he was the Gauleiter's right-hand man. Ernst Kaltenbrunner, head of the Reich Security Central Office in Berlin, which was dominated by the SS, had recommended him for the post because of his Aryan appearance, as Gerdes now told his dinner companions. In April 1945, at the headquarters of the Munich Gau, he had received an order direct from Kaltenbrunner. It instructed Gerdes to work out a plan preparing for the "liquidation" of all the inmates of the Dachau concentration camp, as well as two other camps for Jewish forced laborers in Landsberg and Mühldorf in Bavaria. Kaltenbrunner intended to have bombs dropped on these two outlying camps from the air. The operation was given the name Cloud A1.

"No way was I going to carry out those orders," said Gerdes in Nuremberg. When Kaltenbrunner sent a message by SS couriers that he could expect summary execution if he failed do as he was told, Gerdes made excuses: it was not good weather for flying, aviation fuel and bombs were in short supply. As for Dachau itself, Kaltenbrunner's orders were to have all the Jewish prisoners there "liquidated by poison," said Gerdes. In addition Kaltenbrunner was now planning to march the forced laborers in the other camps to Dachau to be gassed there. That operation was to go by the name of Cloud Fire. First Gerdes prevaricated, deliberately letting things drag on, then he destroyed the papers containing his orders and made for the countryside. "I prevented the gassing of about 120,000 people," he boasted in the Witness House.

When the Americans had taken Bavaria, Gerdes walked into a U.S. checkpoint. He claimed to be a "refugee from the East," was given provisional papers, and found work on a farm. It was unlikely that he would have been identified as a prominent Nazi official if he had not voluntarily handed himself in to testify against Kaltenbrunner. He arrived in Nuremberg one evening and reported to the courthouse, whereupon he was put in a prison cell. However, when he had told his story to a U.S. officer the next morning, he was allowed to move to the Witness House.

Gerdes stayed in Nuremberg for about four weeks and was repeatedly questioned during that time. Finally the Americans decided that his evidence was important in backing up their indictment of Kaltenbrunner. The liquidation of the inmates of concentration camps and prisoners of the Nazis throughout the Reich, ordered by the head of the Reich Security Central Office, was a serious matter. At the Witness House, the countess heard that the interrogations of Gerdes were going to the utter satisfaction of the Americans—"They rewarded him with plenty of cigarettes," noted Kálnoky, who herself was a chain-smoker.

Gisela Limberger left the Witness House just before Christmas 1945. She did not write anything in the visitors' book. It is not clear whether, before leaving, she had any more encounters with Rudolf Diels, whom she admired so much, but presumably he could have opened her eyes a little further to the misdeeds of the Nazis. In many interrogations under oath, the former Gestapo chief had by now proved himself a useful informant to the prosecutors. From the first he denied the claim, very commonly made by both witnesses and the defendants, that no one had known what was going on in the concentration camps. Anyone who was well-informed at the time, Diels thought, could not have been in the dark about "the gassings." He himself, he said, had heard of Zyklon B, described as a means of pest control, at the beginning of the forties. "In 1943 the use to which the gas was being put was known to the general public."

It was also untrue, said Diels, that it was impossible to say no in the Third Reich. He claimed that he was living proof of it. However, Diels the bon vivant, also known in the Rhine area as "the Borgia" because of his lavish lifestyle as head of local government in Cologne, was careful not to mention that he had been under the protection of Göring for a long time. Gisela Limberger had plenty to say about that. In Cologne, besides being involved in various other scandals, Diels had had a relationship with an actress who was well-known locally, and who finally became pregnant by him. Such things were frowned upon in the bureaucracy of the National Socialist Party, and were usually punished severely. Diels, however, was only transferred to Hanover as head of the local district there in 1935.

From Hanover he went on, in 1941, to be head of the shipping department in the Reich Hermann Göring Works, a state company founded at the end of the 1930s. The directorial post he was given was his "dowry" for marrying Ilse Göring, as Diels himself openly admitted. His new position soon opened his eyes to the deportations of Jews then in progress everywhere. Transports were supposed to be crossing the Danube as well. In the Witness House, Diels boasted of having prevented that "because the idea didn't appeal to me." He alleged that several of his colleagues blocked these deportations by water, organizing a traffic jam in the river whenever such transports were about to leave, or so Diels claimed. After that, he said, he sent orders from his office in Berlin for shipping traffic to be temporarily halted.

Diels told these and similar tales of heroism in November 1945, and of course he did not fail to mention that he had spent the last months of the Third Reich in the cellar prison of the Reich Security Central Office in Prinz-Albert Strasse, Berlin. Like many others, he had been arrested after the assassination attempt of July 20, 1944, and was freed from jail by the Allies. Diels soon became one of the key witnesses for the Americans, as U.S. Private First Class Richard Sonnenfeldt remembered: Diels, he said, was extremely valuable, especially in the initial confusion of preparations for the trial: he could provide the Americans with detailed and almost unparalleled inside knowledge of the way the National Socialist regime functioned.

And they urgently needed such details. "You have to understand that there was sometimes a good deal of chaos among the prosecuting team," Sonnenfeldt told me in his deep American voice as he sat by the telephone in his Long Island home. "Basically, we didn't know until the beginning of October just who the defendants were going to be." There had to be a very complex process of coordination. It was not just a matter of building the prosecution case for the first international court ever to put a state and its representatives on trial; every point in the indictments had to be discussed and agreed to by the four prosecuting nations, and they were not by any means always united.

It was late afternoon on Long Island. Sonnenfeldt's house was near a small yachting basin, where the sailboats rocked in the wind like brightly colored scraps of metal. "In retrospect, it all seems to have been so well planned and organized," mused the veteran of Nuremberg, "but the reality was quite different." There had been a good deal of confusion, he says, some of the prosecuting teams had been going ahead independently of each other, others were actually at cross purposes. In one of the secondary trials held later, the prosecutor Kempner was still circulating memos to his colleagues complaining that witnesses were often being produced "although no one knows who asked them to come."

During the trial, organization was in the hands of the General Secretariat of the court. This was where the translation of documents and the summoning of witnesses were organized. The lawyers were always complaining of all the office work involved. Statements made under oath were often not translated in time to be placed before the court when they were wanted, and as a result it was impossible for defense counsel to get certain documents or sworn statements into the records of the trial—only documents that could be read in all the official languages of the trial were allowed. The system for summoning witnesses also broke down continuously. There were witnesses for the defense who could not be found, although everyone knew where they lived; there were witnesses on whose appearance the court did agree, but who did not receive notification, while other people turned up in Nuremberg without being asked to come by anyone. Ultimately no one could say whether there was method in this madness—several of the defense counsel, at least, kept complaining that obstacles were being put in their way.

People also sometimes turned up in Novalisstrasse unasked. A lady called Erna Michaela Ross knocked on the door of the Witness House one day. This woman—"round as a pot-bellied stove," as the countess rather unkindly described her figure— had spent a few days in jail in Nuremberg before being transferred to the villa on the outskirts of the wood. "Why she was here was a mystery to her and everyone else," noted Kálnoky, who began trying to find out from both the defense lawyers and the prosecutors who had requested this lady's presence. She was a teacher and came from Berlin, but she had no story to tell apart from a few experiences of the arrival of the Russians in the bombed-out capital. Ross stayed at the Witness House for weeks, and still no one could explain why she was there and what the point of her staying on was. Finally one day a large limousine came for her. She did not leave the Witness House without inscribing a fulsome verse of some length in the visitors' book. "My thanks are great although my name is small," she wrote, adding a rhyme: "My grateful heart would like to thank you all."

The company assembled for the Nuremberg trials had thinned out considerably by Christmas Eve 1945. The army of journalists had shrunk once the prosecutors began boring their hearers with endless monologues citing document after document. Shortly before Christmas the judges and prosecutors flew home to their wives all over the world, while the German defense lawyers set off for their own homes over potholed roads, making journeys by stages, over a period of several days.

A small Christmas party was organized in the Witness House. There was to be a turkey, for a handful of guests were still there in Nuremberg. Early in the evening Sonnenfeldt and his colleague Lieutenant Wulff turned up with a surprise present for the countess: as well as cigarettes and whisky, they brought a big box containing toy soldiers and other gifts for the Kálnoky children. The soldiers and their little tanks and cannon still bore the emblem of the Wehrmacht—playing with such warlike toys was strictly forbidden to German children in those new days.

Sonnenfeldt had had the toy soldiers confiscated from a private house to use them in questioning a witness. This was General Franz Halder, Hitler's strategic specialist in the Blitzkrieg campaign in France and the Low Countries, and he used the little figures to show the Americans how the Wehrmacht had managed to take Norway, Belgium, and France so quickly. Halder had been chief of general staff of the army, and in the first years of the war he had left his own mark firmly on German battle strategy. After disagreements with Hitler, however, the Führer fired him in 1942, and two years later Halder had been arrested in the wave of arrests following the July plot. In December 1945, now sixty-one years old, the Franconian officer with the short Prussian haircut and round-rimmed glasses sat on the floor beside young Private First Class Sonnenfeldt. "It was a strange scene," says Sonnenfeldt. "There I was playing Blitzkrieg games with a real-life general, using toy soldiers."

The scene was soon repeated in modified form at the Witness House. This time eight-year-old Fárkas, who loved uniforms, and his sister Eleonora sat on the floor, while the generals present issued orders to the toy soldiers from their armchairs.

Father Flynn had brought a Christmas present as well, a nativity scene made of china. The countess in fact thought it was in rather poor taste, and passed it on to Elise Krülle. More important was the fact that the priest had managed to rustle up a typewriter for her. In his spare time Flynn often wrote articles

for the Catholic monthly magazine *The Sign*, of which he had
once been joint editor. The versatile priest had just been writing an article about Nuremberg, in which he described the city
where the military tribunal was being held as "the most tragic
sight in Germany today." He must certainly have encouraged
the countess to write her account of her daily life at the Witness House. Soon she was sitting in her room in the evenings,
typing. She was also given an easel, brushes, and paints for
Christmas. Countess Kálnoky was a talented amateur painter,
and had even colored in the stained glass for several church
windows in Budapest. Now she asked some of her guests to
model for her, although there is no record of what kind of portraits she produced.

Father Flynn could not spend Christmas Eve at the Witness
House himself: as a priest he had to say Christmas Mass twice,
to congregations numbering about 1,400 in all, as his personal
records tell us. Even God's blessing was under bureaucratic
control in the U.S. army, so the priest had to deliver a Chaplain's Report every month. Flynn always filled in the printed
form carefully, and from these forms we can tell that he was
worried about the sexual morals of the troops at this time. His
Nuremberg headquarters was the church of St. Anthony, built
in the Jugendstil. It stood in the Gostenhof area of the city, and
not far from the courthouse building, and as if by a miracle
it had survived the air raids. At the end of October 1945, the
priest married his first German-American couple there. We may
suppose that the two young people had a little addition to their
union on the way, a good reason for going to the altar.

American soldiers could be seen flirting with German girls
everywhere at that time: in the offices of the occupying forces,
in the bars of Nuremberg, in the streets. There was new joie de
vivre in the air, even in the bombed-out streets where the smell

of decaying bodies buried under the ruins still rose in many places.

This feverish outbreak of flirtation seemed to take hold of the city inexplicably, and yet it was not too difficult to decipher. The war was over; a sense of freedom inspired the local inhabitants. In addition, there had probably seldom been so many young people assembled in Nuremberg over a long period as in the months immediately after the end of the war. The members of the occupying forces consisted almost entirely of young soldiers, and once the office staff involved in the trial had also arrived in the city in the fall of 1945, young people were clearly in the majority. The women among them might be shorthand typists or interpreters, newly qualified lawyers, or researchers. Many of the auxiliaries and assistants at the tribunal were under thirty-five, and the number of women among them was unusually high for those days.

Father Flynn kept a stern eye on all these young people. As well as the many services he performed, he gave a lecture on sexual morality once a week after December 1945, drawing an audience of over a hundred at a time. The priest does not seem to have included himself, it would seem, in his moral sermons, for the domestic staff of the villa in Novalisstrasse observed that he was now paying court to the countess more and more openly. His tendresse for her had been the subject of gossip in the whole house for a long time, and only Ingeborg Kálnoky herself did not seem to notice it—at least, not yet.

Early in January 1946, the generals suddenly and quickly left the Witness House. Kessler, Köstring, and the other officers had done little but hang around waiting for a month and a half; now they were given half an hour to pack their bags. Soon after that, Köstring was moved to the witnesses' wing of the courthouse building, while Generals Kessler and Hardy presumably went into safe custody somewhere as well. Lahousen, who no longer had a bodyguard, and Ambassador Rintelen were accommodated in a villa in Fürth, where they were still regarded as prisoners of war, and went for walks together every day.

Lahousen's statements to the court were to be quoted again and again in the months that followed—the prosecutors, however, had no more interest in him personally, and the defense lawyers certainly did not want to hear from the man who had done their clients so much damage. Even Rintelen was soon avoiding the key witness for the prosecution. "He was very strung up, and deeply pessimistic," said the ambassador later in a letter to the countess about Lahousen. "I decided not to go walking with him anymore, because he simply closed his mind to good advice."

BITTER MEMORIES

New guests had arrived. "The man had hardly any teeth left, and he showed me the scars of dog bites on his legs," typed the countess that evening on her new typewriter. For the first time since the opening of the Witness House, she had a former concentration camp prisoner there. She thought he looked pale when he greeted her, very pale. His pitiful appearance alarmed Kálnoky the moment she set eyes on him, and soon she was feeling even more uneasy. How on earth was she supposed to seat this man and Hitler's personal photographer together at the same table?

Kálnoky was so worried that she omitted to find out any more about her new guest. She remembered neither his name nor his age nor the concentration camp in which he had been held. All she could recollect later was that he was "an engineer," and he stayed at the Witness House for some time. Another "former concentration camp inmate," as she described him, also arrived: a farmer from Franconia. Unlike the toothless man, who had been very serious and quiet, the Franconian farmer was bubbling over with the joys of life, as the countess noted—she got on more easily with someone like that.

The farmer immediately started looking for something useful to do. He spoke to Elise Krülle, and soon there was a mountain of children's socks with holes in them piled up in front of him. After that, the countess wrote, he darned the holes her children made in their socks beautifully, evening after evening. This man had been in Dachau, and particularly appreciated the "white, sweet-smelling sheets" in the house, she wrote, adding, "after all his deprivations." However, she probably didn't want to know what evidence he was giving during the day—at least, there is no mention at all of it in her account. Nor did she ask this guest's name. Neither the farmer nor the toothless engineer left any trace of himself in the visitors' book. To this day, then, we do not know who they were, where they hailed from, and what became of them.

But they were not to be the only guests at the Witness House who, for whatever reason, did not feature in the visitors' book. The countess herself was forgetful, particularly over the names of people who seemed to her rather obscure. All she remembered later of another former camp inmate was that he had probably been in Mauthausen. At the time when the witnesses described by Kálnoky were in Nuremberg, several survivors of the camps were in fact staying in the city to give evidence to the court, and several of them came from Mauthausen—it is possible that at least some of those also spent a night at the Witness House.

For instance, Franz Blaha, a Czech medical doctor who appeared as a witness before the military tribunal on January 11, 1946. He had spent four years in Dachau up to the liberation of the camp in April 1945. He had first been assigned to the punishment battalion, then to the medical area. Here the Czech doctor, who spoke fluent German, himself performed about seven thousand autopsies and supervised five thousand more, so he knew a very great deal about the experiments that were made on human beings in Dachau. To give the medical students of Munich practice, for instance, they were allowed to carry out stomach and gall bladder operations or perform liver punctures on perfectly healthy people, operations that sometimes ended in a fatal hemorrhage for the victim. There were also typhoid, malaria, and phlegmon experiments in the course of which a large number of the experimental subjects regularly died. The death rate was particularly high in phlegmon experiments, when healthy individuals had pus injected into their veins or muscles, leading to severe and very painful inflammation or blood poisoning. Some of these people had all their limbs amputated. Sooner or later, most died as a result.

Once they were dead, Blaha said, it was usual to remove their skin. "I was often ordered to do that." Skin from the back and the breasts, he said, was in special demand: "It was chemically treated and then dried in the sun." Afterward these pieces of human skin were used to make riding breeches, gloves, slippers, and ladies' purses. If there was a shortage of skin, people might be killed simply to provide it. The skulls and skeletons of prisoners were also in demand—"In those cases we boiled the skull or the body in a large vessel." Then the "soft parts" were removed and the bones bleached and reassembled. Skulls with good teeth were much sought after. "It was dangerous," Blaha told the court, "to have good skin or good teeth in Dachau."

When it came to the last days of April 1945, the Czech doctor's evidence conflicted on one point with the statements of the former Gau chief of staff in Munich, Bertus Gerdes, who had stayed at the Witness House. Contrary to the claims of Gerdes, Blaha's information was that just before the Allies liberated Dachau, another forty people had been executed there. These were those known as the *Nacht und Nebel* ("night and fog") prisoners, concentration camp inmates who could be allowed no contact at all with the outside world because their very existence must be hushed up. According to Blaha, they were all killed by being shot in the neck and then shoveled into the crematorium.

Blaha stayed in Nuremberg for several days. A thin, pale man with a strikingly high forehead, he spoke perfect German, but by now he hated the language. He had let himself be induced to speak it in the courtroom only because, he said, there were simply no words for much of what went on in the concentration camp except in German—it was, so to speak, the vocabulary of those who were less than human, for which there was "no fitting equivalent in any other language."

At the end of January 1946 the French prosecution team took over the presentation of evidence in the courtroom. The prosecutors called survivors of the Mauthausen, Auschwitz, and Ravensbrück concentration camps to the witness stand. The French prisoner Maurice Lampe described work in the stone quarry in Mauthausen. Exactly 186 very irregular steps led down to it, and once, he said, a group of British, American, and Dutch air force officers had been very painfully killed on this stairway cut out of the rock, when they were forced to keep carrying heavy blocks of stone up the steps. One after another, the men had collapsed, and soon the stairway was covered with blood and corpses, said Lampe. "I almost trod on one man's lower jaw."

A few days later Marie-Claude Vaillant-Couturier came to the witness stand. She was a pretty, slender woman of thirty-three, and wore a suit with a close-fitting jacket and a full skirt. Before her arrest in February 1942 she had worked as a photojournalist, and had joined the Résistance after the German occupation of France. She now sat in the constituent assembly of the French parliament as a communist deputy. In January 1943 Vaillant-Couturier had been taken to Auschwitz in a transport of 230 Frenchwomen; only 49 were to survive the torture. She gave evidence of forced sterilizations and the murder of pregnant women, of working conditions when the prisoners were set to draining the swamps near the camp, and how some of her companions had had their skulls smashed in at morning roll call, purely for the amusement of the guards.

Vaillant-Couturier also described the brothels for SS men in Auschwitz and Ravensbrück, where she had been transferred in July 1944. When the female prisoners had been washed and disinfected, SS men would come along and choose one or another of the naked young women, who were then allotted to them as personal servants. The female overseer told each of the chosen girls to obey her SS man implicitly, whatever he wanted her to do. When industrialists or factory managers came to the camp to recruit laborers, the inspection was not so very different. "It was like a slave market," said the Frenchwoman. "They felt your muscles, asked about your state of health, and then made their choice."

Block 25 in Auschwitz had been the anteroom to the gas chamber, she added. There were often mountains of corpses stacked outside it, and rats the size of cats gnawed the dead bodies. Later, she said, when she had been liberated, she had looked more closely at the gas chambers of Ravensbrück. "The unpleasant smell of the gas still lingered in them," she said. The poison left behind small, pale green crystals that were simply swept up later. In Auschwitz the substance used to kill human beings was a common pesticide for gassing lice, she added. Vaillant-Couturier did not give the name of the poison, but she was speaking of Zyklon B.

When the French prosecutor had finished questioning her, the Nuremberg lawyer Hans Marz spoke. He was representing the Jew-baiter and former Nazi Gauleiter of Franconia Julius Streicher, one of the defendants. Basically, Marz had only one question to ask in cross-examining her: "How do we explain the fact," the lawyer inquired, in a voice that suggested he had detected someone stealing eggs, "that you yourself survived all this so well that you come back here in a good state of health?" Vaillant-Couturier replied, in chilly tones, that she had been freed in the spring of 1945—"A year gives you time to recover."

After her evidence, the young Frenchwoman turned toward the defendants' bench with a vigorous movement that set her full skirt swinging. Then she slowly walked past the accused, looking into the face of each in turn. "I wanted to see what they looked like," she said some years later in a radio interview. Her son made the word-for-word transcript of this interview available to me. It had seemed to her a kind of miracle, she said then, that she, a former concentration camp prisoner, was standing face to face with men like Göring, and that these once-mighty Nazi grandees were now sitting on the defendants' bench, prisoners themselves. The Frenchwoman ascribed the fact that she had been able to give evidence at Nuremberg to her sex. "The prosecutor wanted a woman witness."

Marie-Claude Vaillant-Couturier traveled back to Paris on the day she gave evidence, January 28, 1946, so she had presumably stayed only one night, a Sunday night, in Nuremberg. Whether she spent it at the Witness House is not known. The countess does not mention her anywhere, but that is not necessarily significant, for Ingeborg Kálnoky could sometimes be very reserved and cool with women—particularly pretty young women. Later, Robert Kempner said something suggesting that Vaillant-Couturier may have stayed at the Witness House.

Wherever this particular prosecution witness spent the night, it is certain that the French photojournalist met a Spanish colleague in Nuremberg at that time. This was Francesco Boix, a tall, dark-haired Catalan, aged twenty-five. Boix had been in Mauthausen concentration camp, where he worked in the photographic laboratory. He too must have arrived in Nuremberg that Sunday, January 27, 1946, although his interrogation went on until the following Tuesday. During his stay in Nuremberg the Spaniard took several photographs of Marie-Claude Vaillant-Couturier, which are now in her son's hands. The Frenchwoman herself said later that she had met the young photographer in Nuremberg.

Both spoke excellent German. If they really did stay at the Witness House, then they must have met Heinrich Hoffmann there. Hitler's photographer always took an interest in new guests, particularly those who came from concentration camps, as the countess had observed. In the case of the toothless engineer, according to her account of it, Hoffmann had been quick to ask for details of everyday life in the camps. "Hoffmann wanted some insight into the real life of a concentration camp," Kálnoky noted, "claiming to have no idea about it." On being asked, she says, the engineer spared Hitler's friend no detail.

It is unlikely, of course, that the photographer really wanted to know details, for when talk at the Witness House turned to the concentration camp products in such demand in certain Nazi circles—the shrunken heads made in some of the camps, lampshades manufactured from tattooed human skin—Hoffmann was quick to dismiss these stories, as Kálnoky recollected later. He claimed that "these absurd tales" were nothing new to him; he had already encountered such things recently in the Nuremberg courthouse building. But even before that, Hitler's houseguest and personal photographer can hardly have been as ignorant as he made out. Hoffmann himself had certainly been to Dachau at least once, in January 1943, as recounted in the memoirs of a former prisoner who was obliged to greet him at the time.

At the beginning of the trial in November 1945, the Americans had shown a film with original photographs from the concentration camps. It had shaken everyone badly, even some of the accused. It was discussed in the Witness House. Ingeborg Kálnoky could not help remembering the terrible screams of the thirsty people she had once heard when she and her family, after escaping from Budapest, had taken refuge with the bishop of Györ. For a week, freight trains crammed with human beings had passed through the town every day. You could see a few faces through the little windows of the cattle trucks; those trains were presumably on their way to Auschwitz. That was when Kálnoky first had some glimpse of the barbaric horror that people elsewhere were enduring. Now she learned the whole truth.

Heinrich Hoffmann, however, persisted in denying any knowledge of it. In the Witness House he claimed, and stuck to his claim, that neither Hitler nor he had the faintest idea that there were death camps. Anyway, the photographer never tired of repeating, he'd never taken any interest in politics, he had just been a kind of steadying influence on his friend Hitler, and his photographs—well, they never showed anything political. Close as he had been to Hitler, he was constantly trying to give the impression of having had nothing to do with the crimes of the Nazis. Even the countess gradually came to distrust him, and expressed her suspicion that Hoffmann was trying to conceal something that could make life difficult for him.

There were plenty of reasons for Hitler's personal photographer to make light of his role in the Third Reich. Hoffmann had played a special part in promoting the cult of the Führer. His postcards, his portrait photographs, his volumes of pictures, and above all his booklets of stickers, little pictures of Hitler for schoolchildren to put in their photograph albums, were the perfect means of manipulating public opinion, making their way into all living rooms. Thanks to Hoffmann, Hitler had complete control over his own public image. Not only were Hoffmann and some of his handpicked employees the only people allowed to take photographs of Hitler at close quarters, but through such publications as the *Illustrierter Beobachter*, a uniquely designed photographic magazine considered the illustrated counterpart to the National Socialist newspaper the *Völkischer Beobachter*, Hoffmann made sure that Hitler's politics were presented impressively in visual terms. His mail-order business supplied exclusive "Führer Photos" to the editorial offices of practically every part of the German press. Hoffmann's control over the pictures printed throughout the Reich was almost total.

Hitler's photographer was always at the dictator's service. If there was a picture that Hitler did not think ought to be published, he would tear off the right-hand top corner of the print, and Hoffmann knew what to do about it.

"The camera does not lie," Hoffmann used to say now and then, and perhaps Francesco Boix could have confirmed that remark—although the two photographers would have ascribed very different meanings to that idea. The Catalan saw himself as a reporter of the truth, documenting the living conditions of ordinary people. Boix, from Barcelona, had fought on the Republican side in the Spanish Civil War, and after the victory of the dictator Franco had fled to France, where he volunteered for the army at the beginning of the war. In June 1940 he had been taken prisoner by German soldiers. Instead of going to a POW camp, he was sent to Mauthausen.

Francesco Boix placed photographs from the Mauthausen concentration camp before the court at Nuremberg. They showed such things as a macabre execution scene that, Boix explained, had been accompanied by music from a gypsy band forced to play the melody of "J'attendrai" ("I will wait"). There was also a photograph showing a visit to the camp by the head of the SS, Heinrich Himmler, and Kaltenbrunner, one of the defendants at Nuremberg. They were clearly viewing, among other things, the corpse of a man who had just collapsed and fallen in the stone quarry.

When the prosecutor asked if the photographer recognized anyone he had seen at Mauthausen in the courtroom, Boix turned to look at the defendants' bench and said, "Speer." The architect who became armaments and war production minister had been one of a group of visitors to Mauthausen in 1943, he said. Albert Speer had been wearing a pale suit at the time, and not least because of that, Boix recognized the man in all thirty-six pictures taken of the visit. "He always looked very pleased in the photographs," added the Spaniard.

The witnesses who appeared before the court in person in January 1946 to give evidence of conditions in the Nazi concentration camps were not the only ones asked to attend and answer questions on the subject. Not all of them, however, were summoned to give their evidence in court. It was common for witnesses merely to make statements under oath in one-on-one interviews outside the courtroom, and those statements were then introduced into the trial as documentary evidence. Nonetheless, these witnesses, too, often had to stay on in Nuremberg for a while in case they were needed for interrogation in court after all. For that reason, the entries in the visitors' book in the Witness House cannot always be chronologically matched with appearances in court as the files record them.

As far as possible, and to keep the proceedings in the courtroom from going on too long, the prosecutors presented only those witnesses whose knowledge went beyond the information that could be gained from previous documents. That evidence consisted partly of Nazi records that had been seized, partly of statements made under oath. But of course it was necessary to find out whether a witness might not have more to say than was recorded in the files. Considerably more people, therefore, were questioned in advance than appeared on the witness stand at the trial later. An entire department of the prosecution team was concerned with tracking down potential witnesses, which explains why guests stayed for weeks or even months in Novalisstrasse, even though they never appeared in person at the trial.

This was the case with the Franconian farmer, of whom we know little except that he had been a prisoner in the Dachau concentration camp. Since he made himself useful, darning all the children's socks, he was soon a welcome guest—but he did not even leave his name in the visitors' book at the end of his stay.

However, that too can be explained: guests usually write something in a visitors' book only when they have felt that a place was particularly pleasant. If you do not feel that, courtesy suggests that it is better to make no entry at all. It is difficult to imagine that a former concentration camp inmate would have felt truly at ease in the company of such men as Hoffmann the photographer—however much "light conversation," as she called it, the countess employed to smooth over differences between her guests.

On the other hand, the former Nazi functionaries and Wehrmacht officers do not seem to have been upset by the presence of a few former members of the Resistance in Novalisstrasse. There was a feeling of transition during those days, when the old Third Reich had collapsed and the new Federal Republic of Germany was not yet in existence. The old values still carried weight in people's minds for lack of any definite alternatives—even if the outer emblems of that world, such as the eagle of the Reich, photographs of Hitler, and the swastika, had been hastily removed.

The Witness House was no more than a mirror of its time: what might appear blurred when seen from a distance was visible in focus here. To the adolescent Gerhard Krülle, who kept his eyes and ears wide open to observe what went on in Novalisstrasse, the old order was still clearly perceptible after the end of the war. "The old Nazis were still talking and acting like the masters," he remembers, "and people from concentration camps somehow still felt like second-class citizens." While some of the guests, like Hoffmann, loudly dominated conversation in the evenings, others were hardly heard as they crept quietly around the house. Against this background it is perfectly logical, strange as it may seem, that Hitler's former supporters, fellow travelers, and helpers immortalized themselves in the visitors' book with long texts lamenting their fate, turning to rhyming verse and supposedly humorous sketches, while their victims and adversaries left their names without comment or gave no sign at all that they had been in the Witness House.

Many lines in the visitors' book, however, contain an unmistakable note of bitterness and grief. For instance, one entry was made in March 1946, about two months after the French concentration camp inmates gave their evidence in Nuremberg. The text is in French, but I have been unable to decipher the signature. The countess herself had no idea who might have written it in her visitors' book—at least, when I showed her this entry on my visit to her apartment in Cleveland, Ohio, she could not remember any guest who seemed to fit. Nor is there anyone in the list of witnesses who were questioned at the trial itself to whom the lines can be ascribed.

It may be that the text was written by a fellow countryman of the other French concentration camp survivors, someone who was to be questioned at Nuremberg but was not called to take the witness stand after all. Or it is possible that the lines were written by a French diplomat who was following the examination of Nazi foreign minister Ribbentrop in March 1946. His interrogation concerned the final attempts by the French to prevent the outbreak of war in 1939 through diplomatic channels. Then again, perhaps the entry was made by a German witness using French in order to express something that he could not or would not say in any other way.

The words are set down in a delicate, regular hand with a number of flourishes:

C'est bon d'avoir de beaux souvenirs
Mais c'est malheureux d'être obligé d'en rire.

It's a bitter saying that can be interpreted in more than one way. Literally, it translates as: It is good to have pleasant memories, but sad to be forced to laugh at them.

Nuremberg, May 8, 1945. American soldiers hoist the flag of victory on the spot where the former Reich Party rallies were once held— the war is over.

The old Franconian city of Nuremberg is a sea of rubble, the church of St. Laurence is surrounded by ruins. Slowly life returns to the devastated streets.

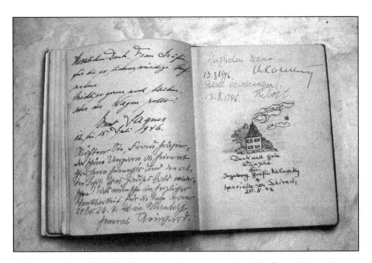

Like a yearbook full of contrasting memories: the first visitors' book from the Witness House in Nuremberg. Top right, two Holocaust survivors have entered their names. Below their signatures is a sketch by Henriette von Schirach.

Employed as a housemaid in her own home: Elise Krülle looked after the comfort of the guests at the Witness House. Her son Gerhard, thirteen years old at the time, observed them. The boy, here in a photograph from 1949, was learning useful lessons.

"She looked like Jean Harlow . . . the beautiful sinner type":
Ingeborg Countess Kálnoky, the first manager of the Witness
House. The Americans appointed her to the post in August 1945.
Aristocratic, with a clean political record, several languages, and
pretty as a picture—she was perfect. The American occupying
forces hired the countess as soon as she had given birth to her
fourth child.

At first sight the villa in Novalisstrasse was a disappointment: small and low-built, a cube with a roof sloping a long way down. But some remarkable scenes were to be played out inside the building.

A regular guest at the Witness House: Hitler's personal photographer Heinrich Hoffmann sorting through his photographs at the courthouse in 1946.

Talented, able to turn any situation to her advantage: Hoffmann's daughter Henriette von Schirach in 1946.

A ladies' man with a scar from his old student fraternity days: the first head of the Gestapo, Rudolf Diels, in the Witness House.

The courtroom on one of the first days of the trial: one of the prosecutors explaining the documentation and structures of the Nazi system.

Hermann Göring on the witness stand at the main war criminals' trial. Before he was questioned, the defendant swore to tell the truth and nothing but the truth. His evidence in court in March 1946 was eagerly awaited.

Robert M. W. Kempner, chief prosecutor in the Wilhelmstrasse or Ministries Trial, here in the courtroom in 1948 with his assistant, Jane Lester.

A tenacious lawyer whose methods of examination were much feared: Kempner in the 1950s.

SS boss Heinrich Himmler in 1933, in conversation with Rudolf Diels, the first head of the Gestapo. Diels left that post in 1934 as the result of a power struggle with Himmler within the Party.

Adolf Hitler and the top brass of the army at a discussion in the Führer's headquarters. On the dictator's right, General Franz Halder, the Blitzkrieg specialist. Later, Halder fell out of favor with Hitler. When interrogated by U.S. prosecutors after the war, he explained his tactics, illustrating them with toy soldiers.

INDECENT ADVANCES

The children were delighted: at last they were rid of the dragon! The dragon's name was Frau Gerschwitz, and it was her job to teach them English. But there was always such a nasty smell of damp dishcloths about their governess. What was more, she couldn't take a joke, and anyway the children didn't think they needed an English teacher. After all, the guards posted out in the street spoke English much better than Frau Gerschwitz, who had a German accent. And the American soldiers *could* take a joke. Fárkas, aged eight, and his sister Eleonora, two years older, sometimes sprayed the GIs with water for fun. If the U.S. guards complained volubly, that was the best way of getting to know more English.

Fárkas and Eleonora did not go to school in Nuremberg. Maybe it was just too difficult to organize, or maybe it was because they were Hungarian citizens and so had no right to a place in a German school. Their mother had hired Frau Gerschwitz so that they would at least learn something, and the governess was supposed to be teaching them French and English. But now, all of a sudden, she had disappeared. That was fine with the children. They said they hadn't been learning anything from her anyway. It was rumored in the Witness House that Frau Gerschwitz had to go because she had claimed that there was something going on between the countess and the American priest.

We cannot know whether Ingeborg Kálnoky sent the governess who was teaching her children English away for that or for some other reason. By now there was so much talk at the Witness House that it was getting more and more difficult to tell fact from fiction, and no one knew whether Ingeborg Kálnoky and Father Flynn were really linked by more than friendship. But the countess was considered an outstandingly interesting subject for gossip. She was pretty, she was on her own, she ran the house. And she had any number of admirers. Many of the American officers who regularly visited the Witness House would have been ready for a little adventure.

There was one incident that ruffled her. It concerned a young lieutenant, as Ingeborg Kálnoky told me in her apartment in Cleveland, Ohio. "He wanted to make me go out with him." The U.S. officer had probably tried some kind of physical lunge at her, amounting to indecent advances. "I avoided him," the old lady told me, "but it was very unpleasant." A day and a half later, as she was sitting on the terrace outside the house with another officer, she had a feeling that the lieutenant whose advances she had turned down was lurking in the bushes, watching her.

It was perfectly conceivable that some of the guests were jealous of the lady of the house. For her part, Ingeborg Kálnoky sometimes organized practical jokes at the villa, and not everyone took them well. She once appeared to the guests in a white sheet, pretending to be a ghost; another time she ran through the house with an open umbrella, terrifying the superstitious Hoffmann. These bizarre attempts to cheer everyone up seem to have been impulsive, made on the spur of the moment. There was an atmosphere of great tension in the Witness

House, and it sometimes discharged itself in strange ways. "It was a time," as the countess later described life in those days, "when you always had the feeling that the ground under your feet was giving way."

But it was also a very exciting time. Elise Krülle herself felt that. There were so many new things to find out, so many interesting people to meet, so much information of which she had never had the faintest inkling to be discovered firsthand. "My mother," Gerhard Krülle told me, "positively blossomed at the time." Elise Krülle had trouble with her leg: an injury that refused to heal up. "She put eggshells on it, she tried all kinds of remedies," Gerhard Krülle said, but still the wound wouldn't heal. "It was a kind of open sore." As for the search for Gerhard's father, they were beginning to abandon hope. A search carried out through the Red Cross had yielded no results, and Elise Krülle had to adjust to the idea of managing on her own with her son in the future.

Until this point Elise Krülle's life had not been particularly eventful. Born in Regensburg, she had met her husband just after the First World War in a hospital where she was working as a volunteer nursing auxiliary. He was a patient in the hospital, one of the war wounded. They did not marry until 1925; Walter Krülle wanted to finish his studies first. Then he found work as an engineer in Nuremberg. By the middle of the thirties they had saved enough money to have the house in Novalisstrasse built. Elise Krülle could never have imagined in her wildest dreams that one day the guests in those four walls would include Hitler's personal photographer, Hitler's adjutant Wiedemann, and Göring's secretary Limberger.

Hoffmann liked to sit in the kitchen, and sometimes even ate his meals there, because, he said, the people in the dining room were "too lah-di-dah" for him. But he probably just preferred the appreciative audience he could expect in the kitchen, for by now some of the other guests were sick and tired of his endless anecdotes about Hitler and Eva Braun. The women in the kitchen, however, lapped up just about every word he said—for instance, his stories about Hitler's way with the ladies: "He laid on the charm for them, you could almost call it gallantry."

But now the time for the defense counsel to have their say in court had come. That meant more witnesses staying in Novalisstrasse, people who, the defendants hoped, would say something positive about them. Göring had called on a Swedish businessman and engineer called Birger Dahlerus, whom he had met in the 1930s. Dahlerus had made contact with Göring again in the summer of 1939, when the Swede was hoping to prevent the war that now threatened Europe on his own initiative. From conversations with British business acquaintances, he had gathered that Britain was not going to put up with a German attack on Poland, which, as Dahlerus saw it, made world war in the immediate future inevitable. The businessman asked for an appointment with Göring so that he could present the situation from the British point of view, and he hoped that the National Socialist government might then be deterred from carrying out their plans for aggression.

Birger Dahlerus met Göring on July 4, 1939, at Carinhall, and in the following weeks he traveled a good deal, working hard on Göring's behalf to set negotiations afoot between London and Berlin. He also organized a German-British meeting on his own country estate in Schleswig-Holstein. Now the former Reich Marshal hoped that Dahlerus would testify to his own activities at the time, confirming the last-minute efforts that Göring claimed to have made to prevent war. In retrospect, however, Dahlerus realized that in 1939 he had merely been used as a pawn in a disreputable diplomatic charade. The facts were that Hitler had always been absolutely determined to attack Poland, but if possible he wanted to keep Britain from coming in on the side of the Poles as a response to German aggression. At the same time, there had been rumors that the British were already preparing a pact to stand by Poland, and the Germans wanted to prevent any such thing.

So Göring had mobilized the Swedish businessman as a kind of special diplomatic courier, aiming to isolate Poland in the international context. On several occasions, Dahlerus carried personal letters between London and Berlin. But all along the Germans were forging ahead with their preparations for war, according to plan. Late in August 1939, Göring spoke to Dahlerus in the presence of Hitler, a meeting that the Swede remembered as distinctly unpleasant. Hitler had such bad breath, he said in Nuremberg, that he had to make a great effort "not to flinch away." Dahlerus had brought news that the pact between Britain and Poland was concluded. At this, said Dahlerus, Hitler had screamed, "If England wants to wage war for a year, I'll wage war for a year; if England wants to fight for two years, I'll fight for two years. If necessary I'll fight for ten years."

During the war, Dahlerus had written a book about his efforts, and it appeared under the title *Last Attempt*. Göring and his lawyer Otto Stahmer do not seem to have studied it closely enough, or they might have guessed that the Swede would not be a good defense witness for Göring. In his book, Dahlerus described the double game that the fat Reich Marshal had been playing with him, culminating in an attempt on the Swede's life. At their last meeting, Göring had said fulsome farewells to Dahlerus. What Göring knew, but Dahlerus did not, was that Foreign Minister Ribbentrop had hatched a plan in Berlin for the plane taking the Swede home to crash. Presumably they wanted him out of the way because he knew too much about what was going on.

However, the plan failed, and Dahlerus lived to tell the whole story in Nuremberg. When the Swede arrived at the Witness House in the middle of March 1946, the countess was struck by his "very well-groomed appearance"—the German guests, whose homes had usually suffered bomb damage, generally looked a good deal shabbier. The Americans had given the Swede a bodyguard, just as they had provided one for Lahousen, and this guard was supposed to sleep in his bedroom. However, Dahlerus was not a prisoner of war, and he did not like the idea of surveillance in the least. Several phone calls were made to the court, but the bodyguard stayed, not just for the new arrival's personal protection but presumably also to keep an eye on him—after all, the prosecutors already guessed that he might be a good trump card for them to play.

Several days passed before the Swede was called to the witness stand. Meanwhile, the usually well-informed radio reporter Gaston Oulmann was on the trail of the way the U.S. prosecutors' minds were working. On the radio Oulmann said that the businessman had better not think he could appear in Nuremberg as a defense witness for Göring. Hearing this remark at the Witness House, Dahlerus flew into a rage and insisted on seeing the General Secretariat. If the report was not corrected, Dahlerus threatened, he would travel back to Stockholm at once without giving evidence. The Swede stayed, and his evidence proved deeply incriminating for Göring. The Americans then allowed him to go to press headquarters in Schloss Stein, where he laid out his position at a press conference that aroused great interest.

Kálnoky, who attended this press conference but had been told to keep as low a profile as possible, registered only "a babble of voices, a band playing, and a colorful medley of journalists from all nations" at Schloss Stein. She obviously took little notice of the sensation caused by the radio report and Dahlerus's statement. Later, she was more likely to remember how Dahlerus would often lecture her at the Witness House, with varying degrees of severity, for smoking too much—"He was always hiding my cigarettes."

The radio reporter Gaston Oulmann was familiar as an institution in and around the Nuremberg courthouse. He was covering the main trial for the Munich and Nuremberg radio stations. Sometimes he commented caustically on witnesses or defense lawyers, but he usually let the prosecutors off lightly. He had disrespectfully described Lahousen, when he gave evidence, as looking like a postal clerk in the suit borrowed from Walter Krülle, missing and presumed dead, and in tones suggesting boredom he described a banker giving evidence about Hjalmar Schacht as "the most dry-as-dust witness to date." Oulmann usually appeared in an American uniform bearing the national emblem of Cuba, as Viktor von der Lippe, one of the lawyers representing the defendant Erich Raeder, noted in his Nuremberg journal. In spite of his rather curious costume, however, said von der Lippe, he spoke "fluent German."

Another prominent defense witness who came to Novalisstrasse was Carl Severing, the former interior minister of Prussia. Small in stature, with a philosopher's high forehead and wavy white hair, he was soon sitting in the garden most of the time and sunning himself, as the countess commented. Now seventy-one, the Social Democrat had been one of the most prominent politicians of the Weimar Republic. Severing was to give evidence on behalf of Raeder, the former commander in chief of the navy, and explain the political background in relation to the Treaty of Versailles. However, he had been brought to Nuremberg far too early, so in practice he had nothing to do but spend hours talking to the lady of the house. She was deeply impressed by Severing: "I have seldom met anyone so well educated and with such wide general knowledge," she typed in her account of that time.

There was a small inn not far from the Witness House, to which several of the guests used to resort in the evenings. The Golden Star was a sandstone building of rather dilapidated appearance in one of the old main roads leading out of Nuremberg. Once, over three hundred years ago, King Gustav Adolf of Sweden was said to have stayed there. Now it was run by a man called Maisel who was well-known for his ready tongue. The place was reasonably well fitted out, and sold watery beer, but sometimes Maisel also had for sale Steinhäger, a brand of gin of the kind that was very scarce just after the war. At times he also served sausage sandwiches off the ration, which made the place very popular.

Hoffmann the photographer was one of the regulars at the Golden Star. Thanks to his good business relations with the GIs, by now he had built up a good stock of various kinds of liquor, and consumed considerable amounts of it himself, but no doubt alcohol tasted better in company. So the witnesses often sat together in the bar during those days of March 1946, a motley collection, including the former police chief of Vienna Michael Skubl; Vice Admiral Walter Lohmann, Raeder's deputy; two former directors of the Reich Bank; and ex-minister Carl Severing. Hoffmann and Severing did most of the talking around the table, as the lawyer von der Lippe noted in his diary. When the evening ended, Hitler's friend and the Social Democrat politician, who had been getting on very well together, were the last to leave, going back to Novalisstrasse in a slightly inebriated condition with a shared key to the front door of the Witness House.

Severing did not get on so well with another of the guests at the Witness House, as the countess was to find out one day. She was standing downstairs in the hall when suddenly she heard loud voices on the floor above. Always anxious to avoid any kind of crisis or conflict, she hurried upstairs. There stood Rudolf Diels on the landing, in his hat and coat. Facing him, standing very upright, was the figure of Severing, who was considerably shorter. "You stabbed me in the back in those days," said the Social Democrat angrily, his cheeks already rather flushed with annoyance. Diels reacted coolly. "Weren't we all doing our duty—as we saw it, from our different points of view?"

Diels and Severing had known each other extremely well in the closing days of the Weimar Republic, and there was an old feud between them dating from that time. Diels had been an adviser under Severing, with the special task of observing communist movements, and in that capacity he had once organized a meeting between Severing's state secretary at the time, Wilhelm Abegg, and two communist members of the Reichstag. When word of this meeting leaked out a little later, not without the connivance of Diels, it served as a pretext to get rid of Severing in 1932, and with him the Social Democratic leadership of the Prussian government—one of the last left-wing bulwarks in an increasingly reactionary Germany.

The Social Democrat had made no further attempts at the time to stand in the way of the right-wing threat fast approaching. Instead, embittered, he retired from politics, while Diels forged his career in the administration of the National Socialist Party. Now, in Nuremberg, Severing had to face accusations that he had done nothing to oppose Hitler. In contrast, Diels had obviously come to an amicable arrangement with the Americans, not least through his connections with his former colleague Robert Kempner. At that moment the former head of the Gestapo was waiting to be collected by a CIC officer. "Maybe you can clear your name with them," Severing snapped as he left, "but not with me." Diels stopped for a moment, as if to say something, but then he hurried down the stairs without another word.

The former Gestapo chief was not going to show any weakness in front of Severing. However, his conscience did prick him over his own behavior in the early thirties. "I always thought I had helped to bring [the Nazi regime] into the world"—that, or something like it, was the way he expressed compunction, several times, under interrogation by the Americans about the early days of National Socialism. Because of his guilty conscience, he had also looked the other way on many occasions when he really ought to have seen clearly what was going on, as Diels said under questioning. In conversation with the Americans, he often wondered aloud whether one man alone could have done anything in particular cases, and the answer he gave himself was always yes. Of course, he said, a departmental head could have quietly disposed of a file now and then. "It depended on your skill."

By this time Ingeborg Kálnoky was really anxious about her husband. She had heard nothing of him for about a year. Of course life was very eventful and varied in the Witness House, so she did not have much time for brooding. Now and then, however, she wondered whether he was still alive. One of the U.S. officers had obtained permission for her to make a phone call to Budapest, which was not easy. The Hungarian capital was in the zone of Russian occupation, and the Cold War, although at first it was hardly perceptible outside that zone, had already begun. The conversation had to be conducted through an intermediary. Kálnoky gave him three numbers, two of which turned out not to be in operation any more. The third number was now that of an office of the Soviet military government. The man who answered the call spoke Russian, and it was useless trying to talk to him.

A few days later, Ingeborg Kálnoky was at her easel in the study when the phone rang. The next moment Elise Krülle came running in. The countess must come, quick, she said, it was a call from abroad. Perhaps from Hungary? Kálnoky sprinted to the phone in the hall. At first there was only crackling on the line, and then suddenly she heard Father Flynn's voice. He was in Rome, the priest shouted into the receiver, and then he was waxing enthusiastic: "A wonderful city!"

Elise Krülle and the other women who kept the household running soon found out who had been calling from Rome. After that, they always claimed that Father Flynn had been summoned to the Pope because of his improper liaison with the countess.

TROUT FISHING AND LADY-KILLERS

The house was hidden behind trees, its windows brightly lit. The Faber-Castells were giving one of their popular evening parties at Dürrenhembach, and this time Ingeborg Kálnoky had an invitation. She saw many familiar faces, representatives of the prosecution and defense alike. Of course Rudolf Diels was there. The former head of the Gestapo was still under house arrest in Novalisstrasse, but through his good contacts with the Americans he continued to find ways and means to escape from his room temporarily. Diels appeared very much at ease with the Faber-Castells, the countess noticed. He seemed to be a close family friend.

A few years ago, Dürrenhembach had still been the Faber-Castells' hunting lodge, but during the war the family had moved permanently into the property. Surrounded as it was by dense woods, it seemed to offer more protection from air raids than their main residence in Stein, near Nuremberg. The atmosphere in the hunting lodge was that of a comfortable, elegant country life. The interior was paneled in dark wood, antlers hung in the hall—the American visitors seemed to love the country-house style. Drexel Sprecher, a member of the prosecution and a distant relative of their hostess, came to Dürrenhembach almost every weekend in 1946. "I always had the corner room on the second floor," he told me, when I visited him in Washington, D.C., in the fall of 2004.

Drexel Sprecher, like other participants in the trial, regarded the Faber-Castells' property as an oasis of peace and calm where guests could relax, playing tennis, riding, or hunting. "In the evenings we ate game hunted on the estate, prepared by the cooks," said Sprecher. "Later we sat in the smoking room over a drink and a cigar, discussing the way things were going." Now and then fish was served at Dürrenhembach, when Sprecher and the master of the house had been catching trout in the streams and pools of the nearby wetlands. They would wade knee-deep through the water, catching the fish near the banks with their bare hands. After the meal there was sometimes a deeply serious discussion on such themes as the "collective guilt" of the Germans, as it was called, or other subjects on which the trial touched. The master of the house and his American guests did not always agree, as Sprecher remembered.

I met Drexel Sprecher in a retirement home on the outskirts of Washington, D.C., into which he had recently moved. Then ninety-one, Sprecher was still an impressive figure. He asked me into the small apartment that he shared with his wife. The old gentleman sat in front of me, ramrod-straight and very tall. Expressive blue eyes looked out from under his bushy white eyebrows. He always kept one eye half closed.

The room contained stacks of documents, many of them from the Nuremberg period. Sprecher had presented the prosecution's case against Baldur von Schirach in the main trial; later he was chief prosecutor in the subsequent IG Farben trial. Like many who were involved in the trials, Sprecher was a bachelor when he came to Nuremberg, and in his spare time he hunted deer and, as he said, "above all women." The American had

met his distant cousin, the lady of the house at Dürrenhembach, Countess Katharina von Faber-Castell, at the beginning
of the 1930s. She was still a teenager at the time, living in Switzerland under her maiden name of Sprecher von Bernegg. Later
the aristocratic young woman went to Berlin, where she soon
had many admirers among the Nazi officers.

"Nina was a very good-looking woman," Sprecher told me
in Washington with a twinkle in his eye. But sometimes, he
said, she had shown a certain taste for the powerful men of
the time. When Nina, an officer's daughter, met Count Roland
von Faber-Castell, it was said to have been love at first sight.
At the time, Faber-Castell already had a divorce behind him.
His first marriage had been to a granddaughter of the Jewish banker Simon Oppenheim, and it was a happy marriage
until the Nazis came to power. In the mid-thirties the National
Socialist Gauleiter of Franconia, Julius Streicher, who had already seized many factories in the Nuremberg area, issued the
count, manufacturer of the famous Faber-Castell pencils, an
ultimatum: either his factory or his wife. Faber-Castell opted
for divorce, and his ex-wife fled to Czechoslovakia.

In 1938 he celebrated his wedding to Nina Sprecher von
Bernegg. However, this private maneuver on the part of the
count—which resembled the defensive strategy in chess known
as castling, when a player moves two pieces at once—did not
keep the Nazis from seizing the Faber-Castell works soon afterward, and the pencil factory was converted to produce munitions. After the war, the count faced what in economic terms
was a heap of rubble.

Meanwhile, the Americans had commandeered Schloss
Stein, the pencil manufacturer's main residence. Faber-Castell
soon found a level on which he could talk to the occupying
forces. "We knew that he had almost been condemned by the

Nazis," Sprecher told me, "so the Americans looked kindly on him." As a cavalry captain in Poland during the war, Faber-Castell had refused to carry out an order to shoot five hundred Jews, and later he was suspected of having connections with the would-be assassins of the July Plot of 1944. After the war, the count immediately made efforts to get his business going again. His wife, Nina, now twenty-eight years old, kept reminding the Americans of her Swiss nationality.

Countess von Faber-Castell was an excellent pianist, happy to perform for her guests at the evening parties in Dürrenhembach. She played the piano at the party to which Countess Kálnoky was invited. The audience in the salon included men like Robert Kempner; Wolfe Frank, the tribunal's chief interpreter; and the Munich lawyer Fritz Sauter, who was defending both the former Reich minister of economics Walther Funk and Baldur von Schirach, former Gauleiter of Vienna. As well as Drexel Sprecher and Rudolf Diels, the company included several of "the locals," as Sprecher called the representatives of Nuremberg society who were happy to accept the Faber-Castells' invitations.

Later, Ingeborg Kálnoky could not be sure who escorted her out to the hunting lodge on that occasion. It cannot have been Lieutenant Wulff, who had been contact officer for both the generals at the Witness House and the lady of the house herself around the New Year, since as Richard Sonnenfeldt remembered, that U.S. officer had left Nuremberg in January 1946. Sonnenfeldt himself, an interpreter for the prosecution, never went to Dürrenhembach—the social standing of a private first class may not have warranted an invitation. Father Flynn, however, could have taken the countess to Dürrenhembach with him; he had a car with a chauffeur available, but at this time the priest was probably still in Rome. In any event, the countess enjoyed the elegant evening at the magnificent country house.

On social occasions, and there were many of those in the Franconian metropolis, Fabian Flynn was always a welcome guest. The priest, who spoke French and German, moved on secular terrain with the greatest of ease. He liked to talk about all sorts of subjects, and took a special interest in politics. Years ago, he had written *A Catechism of Anticommunism* under a pseudonym. In Nuremberg, he sometimes wrote articles for the Catholic weekly magazine *The Sign*, published by the Passionist Order. Father Flynn was always well informed on the political questions of the day, and he had probably also had contact with some of the defendants through the pastoral care that he provided, so he was undoubtedly an interesting and popular conversationalist at that time.

It may be that Rudolf Diels asked the countess a question or two about the priest at Dürrenhembach; he would have had many opportunities to see him in Novalisstrasse. But by this time it was clear to Ingeborg Kálnoky that more than enough had been said about her friendship with Father Flynn, and she would have turned quickly to talk to someone else. The mistress of light conversation was seldom at a loss for words. Moreover, since General Erwin Lahousen's successful appearance in court, the countess was regarded by the prosecutors as someone to be respected, or so Drexel Sprecher told me.

Later that evening Nina Faber-Castell sat down at the grand piano and sang to her own accompaniment. Everyone applauded, but one man appeared particularly taken by the charm of their hostess. Kálnoky surreptitiously observed Rudolf Diels, who was supposed to be under house arrest, for a while, and she found it hard to imagine that there was nothing between him and the lady of the house.

After Diels returned to the Witness House, Countess Faber-Castell had been to visit him quite often. Usually she turned up in the morning and would sit talking to Diels in the living room. Sometimes Kálnoky took her up to the room occupied by Diels, where his pretty visitor would stay for quite a long time. Were the two of them really just talking to each other? These visits gave rise to all kinds of speculation, at least among the domestic staff.

There was a great deal of gossip in Novalisstrasse. In the end, few could distinguish between fact and fantasy anymore. It was into this atmosphere that Father Flynn suddenly resurfaced. Gossip promptly claimed, so Gerhard Krülle remembered, that he had gone to Rome to ask and receive absolution for his sins. However, he had really gone there with a party of U.S. soldiers. A note from March 1946 in the *Passionist Bulletin*, a newsletter published by the Passionist Order, shows that the American officers had been holding discussions with the Italian military bishop in Rome. It is possible that the matter under discussion was Italian priests who had been deported to Germany to work as forced laborers. "Around that time," said Father Fabiano Giorgini, "several deported Italian priests were still reported missing."

When I met Father Giorgini, who died in 2008, he was an elderly man of ascetic appearance with a gentle, friendly voice. He had been in charge of the archives in the Congregazione della Passione di Gesù Cristo in Rome. The monastery of the order, situated in one of the most attractive areas of Rome, just behind the Colosseum, is built on ancient Roman foundation walls, and the monastery archive is kept in the cellar of the extensive building within those walls. Metal filing cabinets standing in long rows contain the history of the order, which was founded in the eighteenth century. The books recording the names of those who stayed the night at the monastery are kept in a wooden cupboard with yellowish glass doors—all the guests of the order are named there, in thick tomes covered with greasy-looking paper. Father Giorgini took the volume for the year 1946 out of the cupboard for me. The guests' names were listed in long rows, handwritten in blue ink—Father Flynn was not among them.

But later Fabiano Giorgini found a note showing that the American priest really did visit Rome in February 1946. According to this information, again provided by the *Passionist Bulletin*, he went to see the Roman church of St. Paul Outside the Walls with the U.S. soldiers. By chance, the group met the American military bishop Francis Spellman there. The two U.S. priests knew each other; only a few months earlier, Flynn had assisted at a Mass being celebrated by Spellman for American soldiers in Aachen. A few days after meeting Flynn in the Roman church, Spellman was to be made a cardinal at the first consistory of the postwar period, on February 20, 1946. For that reason, the U.S. bishop had organized an audience with Pope Pius XII for some of the priests from his region—and on the spur of the moment Spellman included his countryman Fabian Flynn in the invitation. That was how the army chaplain stationed in Nuremberg came to meet the Holy Father.

Flynn's visit to the Pope, therefore, occured in a very different context than that imagined in the wild fantasies of the Witness House. When the priest told her about his adventures in Rome, the countess herself was distracted by quite another cause for concern. Now and then she had been questioned by the American counterespionage service, and this time they were interested in her personally. It is difficult to say for sure whether her name had been blackened by the lieutenant whose amorous advances she had rejected, or whether it was her phone call to Budapest that had aroused suspicion. In any case, she was questioned sternly about her contacts with governmental representatives in Bucharest. She had recently spoken to "Russian sources," a U.S. officer suggested. Kálnoky was easily able to clear herself of that suspicion. But this incident showed that the Cold War was already gathering pace.

Quite late one evening in the spring of 1946, two guests from Switzerland came to the Witness House. One was the American journalist Mary Bancroft, the other Hans Bernd Gisevius, a former member of the intelligence team headed by Canaris. Bancroft must have been the only journalist to set foot inside the Witness House, although strictly speaking she was not really a journalist, since she wrote her reports not so much for the press as for the OSS, the predecessor of today's CIA.

Kálnoky had only one bed free: the second bed in the room occupied by Luise Funk, wife of the defendant Walther Funk, former National Socialist economics minister and president of the Reich Bank. Luise Funk had been staying in the house for a few days. The countess wondered what to do. Then she took Bancroft aside and explained. "I can't really put an American in the same room as a war criminal's wife." So the journalist slept in the children's room, and the countess's children slept with their mother for the time being. Bancroft was grateful, because she did not think she would like Luise Funk, a woman who wore pearl earrings, fine silk stockings, and a strained smile, as Bancroft the intelligence agent observed. Kálnoky did not much like Funk's wife either; she gave the impression that she still thought herself someone special. "She was small, delicate, always suffering from stomach upsets, and she didn't seem to understand what had become of the world these days," she wrote in her account. Kálnoky was relieved when the lady finally left again. "I'll be back," Luise

Funk wrote in the visitors' book—the countess could take that only as a threat.

Meanwhile Hans Bernd Gisevius also presented Ingeborg Kálnoky with problems. The former counterintelligence man made an extremely elegant impression. He wore a well-cut suit and a signet ring, and his cuffs were very white. But when he found out that he was staying under the same roof as one of his worst enemies, he was dismayed. The countess heaved a quiet sigh: once again Rudolf Diels was the bone of contention. Gisevius hated the former head of the Gestapo. They had known each other from the days when they were both students at Marburg an der Lahn, where Diels, so the new guest said, had led a wild life in an ultraconservative student fraternity. Gisevius, who was a little younger, also belonged to this fraternity, known as the Rhenania Strasbourg. Later he worked for a short time under Diels in Berlin. Unable as they were to agree on the aims and methods of the work they were doing, a deep hostility developed between them at that time.

When Gisevius found out that, although the former Gestapo chief was under certain restrictions, he was otherwise able to move about freely, he was consumed by fury. "I'll murder him," he told the countess. Then he fetched a small hip flask from his room and offered her a cognac. Entirely against her usual custom, but seeing the next crisis in the Witness House already looming, Kálnoky accepted a drink.

THE GUEST WHO COUNTED
GOLD TEETH

Hans Bernd Gisevius gave sensational evidence in the court-room. Originally he had been invited to come as a defense witness for the former president of the Reich Bank, Hjalmar Schacht, but the onetime intelligence agent intended to give evidence on much more, and he was asked questions allowing him to do so. Diels had "made the police force a den of robbers," said Gisevius, preparing for a full-scale attack on his enemy, the former Gestapo chief. "Brutal, cynical, and determined to go all the way" was his description of the man. He had not only opened up the Prussian Interior Ministry to the Stormtroopers (SA) and the SS, said Gisevius, he had handed the police department over entirely to the National Socialists who had come to power.

Diels was furious when the countess told him about the inter-rogation of Gisevius in court—and the next moment devoted himself even more intensively to the mosses he was growing on the balcony. In his youth, as he had once told the surprised count-ess, he had been president of a society of amateur botanists from all over Germany. Once spring began he had taken to standing on his balcony now and then, issuing instructions to Elise Krülle as she worked down in the garden. Just then, however, he was giving little thought to his mosses. He called down a wide variety of curses on Gisevius as he watered his little plants.

On the evening of his arrival at the Witness House a few weeks earlier, Hans Bernd Gisevius had given the countess a book that he had just published. Its title was *Bis zum bitteren Ende* (To the bitter end), it was over four hundred pages long, and Ingeborg Kálnoky had absolutely no time to read it. So she passed the tome on to Rudolf Diels, who immediately sat up all night over it. Now the book lay on his bedside table, with hundreds of his own annotations on its pages. Meanwhile Gisevius had already dealt him a second blow with his evidence. Diels was bent on revenge. He borrowed Kálnoky's typewriter, and over the next few days he put together an account that he laid before the court as a statutory declaration. In it, he voiced his suspicion that in his book Gisevius had attacked him so strongly only because he thought "that I had not left the Gestapo prison alive."

But Gisevius had made such a striking impression in court that the agencies were sending out news flashes on what he had to say, although in fact on an entirely different subject. Early on the morning of the day when he was to testify, Gisevius had overheard what struck him a scandalous exchange between two lawyers. Göring's defense counsel Stahmer, in conversation with Rudolf Dix, representing Schacht, had advised him to ask Gisevius as little as possible about the background to what was known as the Blomberg-Fritsch affair, an intrigue presumably instigated by Göring that had led to the resignation of two high-ranking Nazis at the end of the thirties. If Gisevius were to talk about the affair then, Stahmer had told his colleague, Göring would "tell all he knew about Schacht"—it sounded like an unconcealed threat, and Gisevius instantly made it known to the court.

A little later, on the witness stand, he went over the background of the affair as he had already described it in his book.

Werner von Blomberg had been minister of war, Werner von Fritsch commander in chief of the army. Both had been obliged to resign in 1938 on account of private indiscretions, evidently of a delicate nature. Blomberg's crime had been asking Hitler to be a witness at his wedding to a former prostitute; Fritsch was accused of entering into a homosexual relationship. However, the real reason why both men had been removed from office was obviously their critical attitude toward the preparations for war that Hitler was implementing more and more forcefully at that time.

In the courtroom, Hans Bernd Gisevius embarked on long explanations of a kind that the Americans did not really like, and his answers frequently came in the form of the affirmative "*Jawohl!*" a term discredited as a Nazi formula. Nonetheless, the chief prosecutor Robert Jackson had been very happy with this witness, whom he described as the only representative of democratic forces in Germany. Gisevius, who joined the National Socialist Party in 1933, had in fact been a member of the Resistance group that prepared the assassination attempt of July 20, 1944, so he had a great deal of inside information to impart. After the failure of the July Plot, Gisevius saved his skin by escaping to Switzerland, where he had worked in the past as an intelligence agent for the Abwehr.

It was in Switzerland that Gisevius also met Mary Bancroft, ostensibly a journalist, and her boss Allen Dulles, who had run what was probably the most important network of American agents working against the Nazi regime. This encounter, which led ultimately to Gisevius working for the network himself, was probably the main reason why the U.S. prosecutor Jackson showed so much goodwill to the agent; Gisevius had acted as an intermediary between the Americans and the conservative German Resistance.

While Gisevius was trying to exonerate Schacht in the courtroom to the best of his ability, describing the banker as his
"old friend," another of the Novalisstrasse guests appeared as
a surprise witness for the prosecution: Hitler's friend Heinrich
Hoffmann. Schacht claimed that up until July 1932 he had
never publicly supported Hitler and the Nazi Party, but had issued warnings against the danger they represented. And he had
had nothing at all, he said, to do with such figures as Martin
Bormann, head of the Party secretariat, or the founder of the
weekly journal *Der Stürmer*, Julius Streicher, beside whom, to
his annoyance, he was obliged to sit on the defendants' bench
at the beginning of the trial because they came next to each
other in alphabetical order. Robert Jackson now put before the
court a photograph from Heinrich Hoffmann's archives, showing Hjalmar Schacht next to Bormann, with Streicher also not
far away from them in the picture.

Jackson produced a second photograph clearly showing
the president of the Reich Bank giving the Hitler salute. In yet
another photo, he was next to the Nazi propaganda minister
Joseph Goebbels, and a fourth showed him with Funk and
Göring. Jackson came up with nearly a dozen photographs, all
from Hoffmann's archives. The photographer had been busy in
a back room in the courthouse for months, putting his extensive pictorial material in order. Hoffmann did not seem to have
made very much progress with his labors, for the photographs
produced in Schacht's case were undated, which detracted considerably from their value as evidence.

Philipp Fehl described Hitler's former personal photographer as "an elderly gentleman, eager to please, whose courtly
gestures were somewhere between those of a barber and an
orchestral conductor." As a member of the prosecution team,
Fehl had looked through Hoffmann's photographs for pictures

of the men he was to interrogate, and the photographer, he said, had always been extraordinarily helpful in finding the right ones for him. In fact Hoffmann, as it was to turn out many years later, was not just working for the Americans but also lining his own pockets on the side. He obviously absconded with many photographs from his collection, as the Munich art historian Rudolf Hertz proved some years ago. Presumably he took a handful of pictures back to the Witness House with him every day, and hid them among his stocks of razor blades, bars of soap, and bottles of whisky.

Hoffmann probably also showed some of these photos around in Novalisstrasse, including what he said were unpublished pictures of Eva Braun dancing with her brother-in-law, SS Gruppenführer Hermann Fegelein. The photographer once told the countess that he was the sole owner of these photographs, since "I and I alone have the monopoly on them." He liked to sit in the kitchen showing the domestic staff these supposedly secret pictures. How he had suddenly come by so many of them, although he had arrived at the Witness House months ago with practically no baggage, he did not explain—and no one asked.

A new guest arrived at the Witness House, Heinz Max Hirschfeld, a Dutchman. During the German occupation of the Netherlands he had been one of the few members of the Dutch government to remain in office, collaborating with the Germans in the interests of their own country. Hirschfeld had been general secretary of the Dutch Ministry of Economics and Agriculture. In the Witness House, Hoffmann in particular greeted him with enthusiasm. "Remember the good times we had out drinking together in the evenings?" the photographer asked, or something to that effect, according to the account of it given by the countess when Hirschfeld arrived in Novalisstrasse on

May 10, 1946. Evidently this was not Heinrich Hoffmann's first meeting with the Dutchman; he knew his way around the German-occupied countries very well, and had made full use of Hitler's expansionist policies to open branches of his photographic company everywhere.

The Dutchman was less pleased to meet Hoffmann again. There was also another guest at the Witness House whom Hoffmann would have known: Franz Hayler, a state secretary in the Reich Ministry of Economics. Hayler and Diels were the only two guests under house arrest in Novalisstrasse. It surprised a good many people that Hayler was not accommodated in the prison wing of the courthouse—after all, he had been an SS general, and in very close contact with Oswald Pohl, the man who had organized the systematic theft of the possessions of concentration camp inmates. Later, in one of the subsequent trials, Pohl was to be sentenced to death.

Heinz Max Hirschfeld briefly observed the scene at the villa, and half an hour later had himself connected by phone to the court to order a driver to collect him from the Witness House at once. He was not going to spend so much as a single night under the same roof as all those old Nazis.

We do not know where Hirschfeld did stay after that, until he testified on May 14, 1946. He opted to speak to the court in German because, he said, it was the foreign language he knew best. However, his entry in the visitors' book in Novalisstrasse was in English—which may have been another sign that he was distancing himself from the place entirely.

A few days after this incident, an apparently nondescript civil servant arrived in Novalisstrasse. At first Kálnoky did not even notice the man among her crowd of guests, he appeared so pale, subservient, and inconspicuous as he went around in the Witness House. Albert Thoms was the very image of the stereotypical bank clerk whose outward appearance would be instantly forgotten. The parting in his hair could have been drawn with a ruler, he was a weedy figure, and he spoke very quietly. Even on the witness stand he was to maintain this subservient attitude, always speaking in his testimony of this or that personage as "Mr. President" or "Mr. Minister." But what Thoms had to say about the involvement of the top personnel of the Reich Bank, and the former Nazi minister of economics Walther Funk himself, in the worst crimes of the Nazis was devastating. The banking official provided information about "Jew gold," as it was called, the bank deposits from concentration camps consisting of the final valuable objects that had been taken from Jews on their way to the gas chambers.

Albert Thoms, who held the rank of Reichsbankrat (Reich Bank adviser), had been responsible for managing the items made of gold and other precious metals in the vaults of the Reich Bank headquarters in Berlin. He had remained loyal to the bank until the end. After the war, the Americans tracked him down to a salt mine in Thuringia. On the instructions of his superiors, Thoms had moved to the catacombs of the Merkers Mine near Eisenach months earlier, taking with him all the gold and other valuable metal items deposited in the Reich Bank. He obediently remained there, surrounded by sacks full of jewels, wedding rings, and gold teeth, until the Americans found him.

All his life, Thoms had been a dutiful bank official in the senior ranks of the civil service. He had never asked himself any questions about the orders he received from his superiors, even when, in August 1942, he was summoned to Emil Puhl, who was standing in for Funk, the economics minister, as acting president of the bank. Puhl informed Thoms that he could expect deliveries of certain "rather unusual valuables." They were in the form of gold, silver, and foreign currency, but also jewelry and other items. These deposits, the property of the SS, were to be placed in trust with the bank. Finally, Puhl instructed Thoms not to mention the matter to anyone—it was strictly confidential.

On August 26, 1942, Thoms received the first consignment, delivered in a truck by an SS man named Bruno Melmer. Thoms, intent upon proper bookkeeping, asked to what account these items should be credited, to which Melmer replied that the proceeds were to go into an account in the name of "Max Heiliger" for the benefit of the Reich Finance Ministry. Soon more and more SS trucks were rolling up. Unpacking the crates that had been delivered, Thoms and his colleagues stared in surprise: they might have expected the gold and silver coins, but there were also valuable pieces of jewelry, diamonds, vast quantities of wedding rings, gold-rimmed glasses, and finally little nuggets of gold that had obviously come from dental fillings.

In order to count and value these items, the officials of the bank spread them all out on long tables in the bank vaults, and therefore, said Thoms in Nuremberg, "they could be seen by anyone who came into the strong rooms." Puhl often looked in, and Thoms had also told him about the contents of the consignments. Once, for instance, there had been twelve kilos of pearls among the valuables, said Thoms, and he "told President Puhl that I had never seen such an unusual quantity before in all my life."

The deliveries kept coming. In all, Thoms told the court, about seventy-seven consignments were received. "The number of gold teeth grew to extraordinary proportions." Early in 1943 a bundle of bank bills fell into his hands, clearly stamped

"Lublin,"* and another time he read the inscription "Auschwitz." Thoms and his colleagues had a vague idea that these place-names denoted concentration camps, so they asked their superiors "what it was all about." However, said Thoms in Nuremberg, they received no answer, "and we asked no more questions." No written records of these deliveries had been made at the Reich Bank, remarked Thoms at the end of his evidence. "It was all very unusual."

Thoms testified in court on May 15, 1946, stayed another night at the Witness House, and did not leave until the next morning. It may be that the countess exchanged a few friendly words with him that evening—at least, the bank official left an entry in the visitors' book thanking her effusively for welcoming him "with true kindness and the most understanding sympathy." Later, Kálnoky could not remember the man, and she had far more prominent guests to be looked after in the house. Only recently, for instance, the former state secretary in the Foreign Ministry, Ernst von Weizsäcker, had arrived in Nuremberg.

Previously, as Raeder's defense counsel von der Lippe mentioned in his diary, there had been a little political tug-of-war among the diplomats. Ernst von Weizsäcker, who had been German ambassador to the Holy See since 1943, had decided to stay on in Rome after the end of the war, fearing, not entirely without reason, that he might be interned in Germany—after all, he had at one time been Ribbentrop's right-hand man, and Ribbentrop was now conspicuous among the defendants. He had been invited to stay on in Rome for the time being as a guest of the Vatican State. "He had an apartment in the Palazzo

---

* Lublin was the concentration camp in Poland also known as Majdanek, one of the death camps.

San Carlo, where the father confessors also stayed," Cardinal Paul August Mayer told me.

Mayer, a Benedictine priest who was thirty-four at that time, often visited the former ambassador. "Weizsäcker invited us to lunch in the Vatican." When I visited the cardinal in the fall of 2004, he was ninety-three years old, and sat in his sparsely furnished apartment not far from St. Peter's Square, a tall, lean, ramrod-straight figure. A smile came to his old face as he told me about Frau Weizsäcker. "She always thought I looked like her son, who had fallen in the war." Weizsäcker usually spent the morning in the Vatican library, marveling at the church state's inexhaustible stocks of books, and in the afternoons he painted watercolors in the Vatican Gardens or St. Peter's Square.

In the midst of these peaceful occupations he received a request from Nuremberg to appear as a defense witness for the defendant Grand Admiral Raeder. Weizsäcker was not disinclined to do so, but he still feared internment. Consequently the defense lawyers requested safe conduct for him. At first the court authorities rejected this request, but then suddenly anything seemed possible, and Weizsäcker was even allowed to visit his relations in Lindau before he appeared in court to testify. He arrived at the Witness House on May 3, 1946, left his things in his room, and joined the usual company of witnesses and defense lawyers at the Golden Star inn that evening.

Weizsäcker was not called to the witness stand until three weeks later, but then he created a minor sensation. For some time, various defense lawyers had kept bringing the conversation in the courtroom back to a secret additional file that had to do with the pact between Hitler and Stalin in 1939. In this document, which was attached to the nonaggression pact itself, Germany and the Soviet Union had already divided up the entire territory of Poland between them.

The contents of the agreement, which had not been known until this time, were considered incendiary, for they might constitute evidence that one of the powers sitting in judgment, the Soviet Union, had itself been guilty of an offense against international law. The Russian prosecution team made great efforts to come up with more and more arguments to fend off any kind of question about the additional file. And they had been successful—until Ernst von Weizsäcker took the stand. The former state secretary could remember the contents of the file in detail, and now it could no longer be denied. The document did exist.

In the courtroom, the subject was soon changed, but the visitors staying at the Witness House heard all about it again on the radio that evening—they had, as so often, gathered around the large Telefunken radio set in the study. The countess noted later, in her account, that when Weizsäcker heard his recorded voice on the program he was furious. "But that's not me," he kept repeating, "that's my brother's voice." The next morning the diplomat said good-bye with a quotation from Goethe's *Iphigenia*. "Good deeds, not guests, bring every blessing here," he wrote in the visitors' book.

It was on one of those days in May 1946 that Henriette von Schirach dropped in at the Witness House. This was not the first time she had visited. Since her release from the internment camp at Bad Tölz in early March she had visited her father quite often. Henriette von Schirach was "a very striking woman," as the countess noted, not because of her rather round face, but because of her hair. It was auburn, and "reminiscent of the pictures of the old masters." In addition, she always wore pastel colors, spoke very softly, and could thus, in the countess's opinion, "easily appeal to the protective instincts of men." But the thirty-three-year-old's hands, Kálnoky observed, "seemed to have a life of their own, with its own laws." They were always fidgeting with something—her blouse, her purse, her gloves. Evidently Henriette von Schirach was very nervous.

The daughter of Hitler's photographer Heinrich Hoffmann usually turned up accompanied by American officers, and she obviously lacked for nothing. She brought large quantities of cigarettes for her father, who himself did not have to resort to goods sold under the counter, and she also provided him with alcohol. It may be that her powers of attraction for the U.S. officers also owed something to the fact that she was considered one of Hitler's intimate circle. When she was a little girl the future dictator used to do gymnastics with her, chose books for her to read, and even looked over her homework. No wonder she idolized him uncritically.

This time she had presumably come to Nuremberg to support her husband, whose interrogation by the prosecution began on May 23, 1946. On that occasion Ingeborg Kálnoky herself visited the courtroom for the first time. Also present at the trial that day was the Argentinian writer Victoria Ocampo, who wrote an article about it. Baldur von Schirach, as she described it, spoke at length about the Hitler Youth, his alleged home of choice in Weimar, and his love for Germany's great national poet, Wolfgang von Goethe. At a private gathering that evening, one of the judges commented tartly on Schirach's remarks: "No one blames him for venerating Goethe, we blame him for burning the works of Heine."

The judges had repeatedly interrupted Schirach's long lecture, for the point at issue was not any youthful misdemeanors he might have committed, but what he had done in his adult life. However, even when Schirach got around to speaking about a visit to the Mauthausen concentration camp, he stuck to the subject of culture. There had been a symphony orchestra playing in the camp, he said, and a singer with an excellent tenor voice. He claimed to have seen nothing of the terrible stone quarry and the cliff from which many concentration camp prisoners had fallen to their deaths.

Henriette von Schirach was not the only woman to be a frequent visitor to the Witness House, which she called, with flattering exaggeration, "a prison for gentlemen." Her stepmother, Erna Hoffmann, the photographer's wife, was often to be found there as well. She had no official permission to stay at the Witness House, but she still took part in everything except meals. She had enough to eat herself anyway. Countess Kálnoky always wondered where that rather plump lady found all the delicious things that she stored in her husband's room. The Hoffmanns obviously had an enviable talent for getting by extremely well, everywhere and anywhere.

SKELETONS IN THE BIRCH WOOD

It was the middle of the night when the countess was woken by a sound. Had someone just knocked on her door? Alarmed, she sat up in bed and listened. "Please come, Countess Kálnoky, quick!" With one leap, Kálnoky was out of bed and opening the door. There stood Erna Hoffmann, apparently quite beside herself. "My husband . . ." she stammered. "Something's happened." Kálnoky threw a coat around her shoulders and hurried with Erna to Hoffmann's room, which was diagonally opposite hers on the other side of the corridor. The star photographer was hanging just above the floor, his face was blue, and he had a belt around his neck with one end attached to one of the bedposts.

"A knife! Scissors!" Kálnoky cried at once. Erna Hoffmann hastily rummaged through her husband's things, which were scattered about on the table and chairs. Bars of soap lay next to his dirty shorts—her husband had left his room in total disorder. Finally she found a pair of scissors in the general muddle and, with trembling hands, passed it to Kálnoky. Luckily the belt was very narrow and already quite well stretched, but all the same it was not entirely easy to cut through the leather. Kálnoky applied the scissors and exerted all her strength. Soon the belt broke, and Hoffmann's head bumped on the floor. The two women tried to heave him up on the bed, but that seemed to be impossible; his body was too heavy. So they just put a pillow under his head.

Heinrich Hoffmann uttered a sigh, his chest moved, and he began breathing irregularly. The countess felt his pulse. It was weak, but stable. "He needs a doctor," Kálnoky said. "No, no," Erna Hoffmann quickly objected, "that will only make trouble for everyone." They didn't have to say exactly what had happened, suggested the countess. But the next moment the red mark on Hoffmann's throat caught her eye. They would probably have difficulty explaining that to a doctor. "I think he's rather better already," said Hoffmann's wife, and pointed to the table, where an empty cognac bottle stood. "He probably had a bit too much to drink."

Erna Hoffmann had not spent the evening with her husband. Instead, she had gone to the inn after supper with some of the others staying at the Witness House. Later in the hall she had met Rudolf Diels, who had just been brought back by a CIC officer. The two of them talked for a little while. Erna Hoffmann, as the countess had already noticed, appeared to find the former Gestapo chief irresistible. Heinrich Hoffmann suffered torments of pathological jealousy, always fearing that his doll-faced wife, who was about twenty years his junior, could leave him one day. Was that why he had tried to put an end to his life?

Presumably the photographer also had other problems weighing on his mind. Kálnoky had noticed that he suffered from mood swings; sometimes he was on top of the world, at others in the depths of gloom. For years he had consumed enormous quantities of alcohol, and malicious tongues therefore sometimes called him not the official Reich photo-reporter, but the official Reich drunk. While under arrest he had been temporarily obliged to abstain, but since he had set up such a flourishing trade with the GIs there was drink in abundance again. In addition, and despite his conspicuous show of optimism, Hoffmann was probably also anxious about the future. He had certainly found himself a niche at the Palace of Justice with his photographs, and he could set aside a few that he hoped to sell for a good profit later—but much could still happen before he really found his feet again.

Countess Kálnoky decided to keep this incident to herself. She did not want it known by the CIC officers, in particular. However, when she took breakfast up to Rudolf Diels in his room, he looked at her with a remarkably knowing expression. "Anyone might think you'd had a bad night," he greeted the countess. Kálnoky tried to give toothache as an excuse, but Diels just shook his head. "Something the matter with Hoffmann, was there?" he asked, very much in the manner of the police officer he had once been. Of course the nocturnal comings and goings out in the corridor had not escaped his notice, and he had worked out the rest of it for himself.

"Our American friends will be sure to find it interesting," he pressed her further. Kálnoky sat down for a moment at the little table where the breakfast tray stood and groaned, "Please don't breathe a word of it to them!" Then she leaned back in her chair and took a deep breath. "Do you know what the U.S. officer told me to do when he gave me this job in the Witness House? 'Keep things running smoothly,' he said." She quoted her instructions as they had been given to her, in English. And now, Kálnoky went on, she had crisis after crisis on her hands. "The Americans," said the countess thoughtfully, "probably have no idea at all what goes on here."

Diels slowly filled his cup with coffee. "Oh, I assume they have a record of every word spoken in the house." Kálnoky looked at the former police chief in alarm, but he merely shrugged his shoulders. "Putting myself into the Americans' place," Diels went on, "I would naturally have installed a bugging system here before you moved in."

For a moment Kálnoky felt stunned. It had never occurred to her that the Americans might have bugged the house. She still couldn't really imagine it. After all, why were the CIC officials always asking her questions if someone only had to press a button to listen in on a tape recording? In addition, counterespionage agents had carried out all kinds of investigations. Even Diels, who seemed to be on such good terms with them, had his room searched regularly. On the last occasion, as he now added, they had taken the document that he meant to give Kálnoky for her account of the Witness House away from him, along with other things. Diels had written about himself in that document, and the countess had glanced at it briefly while it was still unfinished and before it disappeared—"A man who gives women something to think about," ran one of the sentences that had stuck in her memory.

Kálnoky was deep in thought. Suddenly she heard herself asking a question that she would probably never have voiced in other circumstances. "Doesn't it bother you that all your flirtations might become public knowledge now?" Diels merely grinned and replied nonchalantly, "Oh, that's just part of me, the way your aristocratic title is part of you." However, the countess persisted: there was a lot of talk in the house about his relationship with Countess von Faber-Castell, she said. "That lady is a frequent visitor here," she added rather sharply. "Oh, Maize Countess, could you by any chance be jealous?" Diels asked back, obviously amused. "And then there's Father Flynn, whom we all value so highly—what's he doing these days?" he inquired in the next breath, adding, "I don't know why, but it's been a long time since he put in an appearance here."

Kálnoky rose to her feet abruptly, took the tray, and went to the door. But she turned once to look back. "That's exactly what I mean. Gossip can be rather uncomfortable—and sometimes it's wide of the mark as well."

A pretty blonde woman of about thirty had come to the Witness House: Else Krüger, private secretary of Nazi Reich leader Martin Bormann. Bormann, head of the secretariat of the National Socialist Chancellery, with the rank of a minister of the Reich, was listed as one of the defendants at the military tribunal, although it was presumably some time since he had been in the land of the living. Fräulein Krüger had been summoned to Nuremberg at the end of June 1946 to give evidence on that subject. "An amusing girl," Countess Kálnoky wrote in her account, "and probably much more intelligent than she made out." Krüger had been in the Führer's bunker when Hitler committed suicide, and the rest of the guests at the Witness House bombarded her with questions. Kálnoky herself would have liked to hear more about Hitler and Bormann, who was said to have had great influence on the Führer in the last years of the regime. But Fräulein Krüger was steadfast in declining to talk about her boss, not even uttering commonplaces. Kálnoky thought that she seemed to want to conceal something.

Else Krüger had stayed in the Führer's bunker until the last moment. She was present on April 22, 1945, when after a discussion with the generals Hitler spoke to his close circle of employees, his eyes dulled, and said, "All is lost, hopelessly lost." Then he is said to have kissed his mistress Eva Braun on the mouth, as his secretary Traudl Junge wrote in her memoirs. Krüger got together with the slightly younger Traudl, since none of the secretaries really knew what to do now. "In my mind I was preparing myself for death," said Else Krüger in Nuremberg.

They had stayed on for days in Berlin, in the bunker under the Chancellery, while Hitler married Eva Braun and shortly afterward committed suicide with her. They all heard the shot that broke the silence in the bunker on April 30, 1945—Hitler had shot himself in the mouth.

On the evening of May 1, 1945, Krüger and a few of the other secretaries tried to escape from the bunker. Going by tortuous underground ways through the vaults, they reached the coal cellar of the new Reich Chancellery, where a number of men were standing around ready for flight. Krüger recognized Bormann among them. "Well, good-bye, then," he said to her, according to her statement in Nuremberg. Then she and a group of about twenty other people had climbed up to the exit from the Chancellery and into Wilhelmsplatz. A dead horse was lying in the road, and hungry people had already been hacking off pieces of the animal's body.

Passing through the subway entrance outside the ruins of the Hotel Kaiserhof, the group had made its way along underground passages to Friedrichstrasse Station. Fierce fighting was in progress there. Fräulein Krüger and the others ran through the rubble of bombed-out buildings and finally found shelter in a bunker, but later Bormann's secretary could not remember its precise location. An SS Gruppenführer whom Else Krüger had seen earlier with her boss Martin Bormann turned up at a late hour. He had a severe leg injury. "There are bodies everywhere," he called out to the secretary, saying that his companions were all dead—presumably including Bormann.

That was all that Fräulein Krüger could say in Nuremberg about the Reich leader and anywhere he might be. The judges were disappointed that there was still no proof of Bormann's death. A few days later, therefore, they asked Erich Kempka, Hitler's former chauffeur, to take the witness stand. On the evening of May 1, 1945, he had met Bormann on the Weidenhammer Bridge directly behind Friedrichstrasse Station. Under cover of several German tanks, Bormann, Kempka, and several others had tried to cross the bridge on foot, said the chauffeur. But suddenly the tank beside which Bormann was walking was hit and blown sky-high. "I saw a jet of flame where Martin Bormann had been walking," Kempka told the court. "And I saw something else moving, like a kind of collapse, but it could have been something flying into the air."

According to his own account, Kempka had been within a few yards of Bormann at this point. He himself lost consciousness, he told the tribunal at Nuremberg, and later crawled away. However, presumably the course of events was not exactly as Kempka described it. The body of Reich Leader Martin Bormann was not to be found until the 1970s, when his remains were located near the Invalidenbrücke in Berlin, and could be identified beyond any doubt. Bormann had obviously bitten on a cyanide capsule and ended his own life through poison. For decades, there had been all kinds of rumors about his possible hiding place. Richard Sonnenfeldt was in charge of Kempka at Nuremberg, and he suggests that the chauffeur indirectly encouraged the formation of legends. "We somehow got the impression that he wasn't telling us all he knew," said Sonnenfeldt.

At last a really handsome man turned up to stay at the Witness House. "Tall and elegant, graying at the temples, and with a very charming manner," wrote the countess. Friedrich Ahrens obviously appealed to her. The colonel, a man of around fifty, stayed for just under four weeks at the Witness House, and only the devout cleaning lady disapproved of him: when he undressed, he used to hang his clothes over the outstretched arm of a statue of Christ that stood in his room. Formally, Ahrens was a free man, yet since his arrival Soviet military vehicles had suddenly been posted outside the Witness House. The Russians considered the German colonel the prime suspect in one of the most terrible crimes committed in the final years of the war: Friedrich Ahrens, so the Russians claimed, was responsible for the Katyn massacre and thus for the murder of around eleven thousand Polish officers.

But at the time the Soviets were not sure that their accusations would stand up before the international tribunal. They would have liked to bring Colonel Ahrens before a Russian court, where he could have been tried and condemned without reference to any democratic principles of justice. His appearance as a witness at Nuremberg only delayed the trial unnecessarily, they thought. So a bitter struggle developed behind the scenes in the courtroom for custody of the witness Ahrens. The Soviet prosecution team made several attempts to prevent him from giving evidence, but the German defense lawyers, and not least Ahrens himself, joined forces to insist on his interrogation in court.

The presiding judge alone decided on the framework of the trial, sometimes allowing the defense lawyers five witnesses, sometimes asking only for affidavits, statutory declarations for the purposes of the trial. Actual bargaining at times like this over the appearance of individual witnesses before the tribunal showed how uneven the balance of power was at Nuremberg. While the prosecutors could call on practically any witness they wanted, keeping that witness's identity secret from the defense until the last moment, defense counsel had to hand in laboriously reasoned applications to call witnesses long before the day came for questioning them, and those applications were often refused. The defense could hardly ever prepare ahead to cross-examine prosecution witnesses, since they seldom knew in advance who had been asked to give evidence.

When the trial touched upon the mass shootings at Katyn, the situation for both sides was comparatively fair at the out-set: the defense and the prosecution could present three wit-nesses each, and only the Russian prosecuting team had the privilege of not having to announce the names of their wit-nesses in advance. Two witnesses for the defense, Friedrich Ahrens and Lieutenant Reinhart von Eichborn, stayed in the villa in Novalisstrasse; the third, a general, was presumably held in the Nuremberg prison wing of the courthouse building.

Friedrich Ahrens had asked the countess for paper and pen-cils on the evening of his arrival; he wanted to draw as ac-curate a sketch as possible of the terrain. Kálnoky got out a large drawing block and offered him her watercolor paints to color his sketch. The colonel had been in command of a signals regiment, and had his quarters about twenty-five kilometers west of Smolensk in the village of Katyn. At the time he was living in a grandly furnished property on the banks of the river Dnieper, a house with its own cinema, a shooting range, and several swimming pools—"We called it our little castle on the Dnieper."

One day in the winter of 1942, Ahrens observed a wolf run-ning through the group of birch trees outside this little castle. A wolf so close to the big city of Smolensk? Taking a tracking expert with him, Ahrens followed the trail, which had indeed been left by a wolf. There were also places, on a hill with a birchwood cross on it, where the snow on the ground had been scraped up. Not until spring, when the ground thawed out, did bones come into view, bones that the foraging wolf must have left. Human bones.

At first Ahrens thought it was a grave for the fallen, and he decided to inform the organization in charge of war graves. Months later, however, and on closer investigation, it turned out from letters and scraps of diaries found with the bones that the skeletons must be the remains of Polish soldiers. Some of the local inhabitants confirmed to Ahrens that there had obviously been mass killings in the little wood in the spring of 1940—the locals had heard "a lot of shooting, and screams," said Ahrens.

The colonel had to wait for some while at the Witness House before appearing in court. He killed time by going out to the Golden Star with the other guests in the evenings. These days a man who had not previously frequented the inn was often seated at the next table. One evening this man spoke to the colonel, introducing himself as a "representative of the Russian press," as the countess remembered. They talked about this and that. Later, on the way home, Ahrens had a vague feeling that someone was following him. Fortunately he was not alone. The next day he reported the incident to the General Secretariat of the court, whereupon he was promptly forbidden to leave the villa again before appearing in court—his life might be in danger.

At this time Ahrens's wife was stranded in the Russian-occupied zone, and it had been a long time since the colonel had heard from her. "Perhaps the Russians have already been to see her," he once said anxiously to the countess. Against such a background, the consequences to his family of his statement in court were unpredictable. However, the colonel seemed determined to clear his regiment of the accusation of murder. His moment came on July 1, 1946. Ahrens placed before the court two maps that he had drawn himself. The little wood, the little castle, the river, the town—they were all there in attractive color, and the birchwood cross was also visible. Ingeborg Kálnoky had colored in the colonel's drawings for him, as she proudly remembered later. "Who would ever have thought that my little artistic talent, unworldly as it was, would one day play a part in the documentary evidence of the International Tribunal in Nuremberg?"

As well as the main grave beside the birchwood cross, smaller burial places had been found at Katyn, and as she explained to me, Ahrens had "indicated them with a few little dots" in his sketch. Bodies had also been discovered there, now consisting mainly of "skeletons that had fallen apart." They were, said Ahrens, the "skeletons of men and women," and he explained that "even as a layman I could tell that very well, since most of them had rubber boots on, and the boots had been preserved intact."

After Ahrens had given evidence, the Russian prosecutor made another unconcealed threat to the colonel. Did he know, he asked, that the Soviet state investigating committee considered him one of the main perpetrators of the massacre? Ahrens merely nodded. However, his account had been given a favorable hearing by the other nations represented at the tribunal. The accusation that representatives of the Wehrmacht now on the defendants' bench were responsible for the Katyn massacre was not upheld in the verdicts. Only decades later, after the fall of the communist regime,* was it admitted that the Soviet Union had been responsible for the slaughter in the birch wood.

Friedrich Ahrens left the Witness House on July 5, 1946, with, as he wrote, "the most sincere good wishes to you, Countess Kálnoky, and your charming children." This entry in the visitors' book moved Kálnoky. From all she knew of Ahrens, he was in an even more desperate situation than she was. It was not just that he missed his wife—he had no idea

---

* In 1990, and thus just after the 1989 fall of the communist regimes throughout Eastern Europe in a domino effect

how his children were. The countess often thought about the colonel, whose appearance in court had impressed her. Now and then, however, she abruptly dismissed such thoughts and, feeling like playing cards, went to the children's room, to see if she could persuade the nursemaid Cuci to play a game with her. Cuci did not need any persuasion, since she herself had a passion for cards.

Meanwhile, the courtroom was gradually but inevitably turning into a citadel of boredom, as the English writer Rebecca West acutely remarked. The prosecutors read out countless documents in never-ending monologues, while the defense did just the same with even more frequency. But the judges were beginning to press for results. They decided to distinguish between the prosecution of individuals and that of the various criminal organizations—from the SS to the Wehrmacht—and to have witnesses intended for the latter interrogated in parallel to the main trial, in a gymnasium that was part of the courthouse complex. As a result of this measure, the Witness House soon felt like Times Square. The guests kept changing. Former SS men alternated with trade unionists; rather elderly representatives of the archreactionary Stahlhelm League could now meet members of the Communist Party in Novalisstrasse; people who had worked for the feared security service of the SS met startled antifascists, who could hardly believe their eyes when they saw all these guests mingling freely.

"At the time," mused the countess, when I met her and talked to her in the mid-nineties in the United States, "the Witness House was the only place where these entirely different worlds came into direct contact with each other." She readjusted her pearl necklace and turned her eyes to the television screen that flickered in the background of our conversation.

A NEGLIGEE TOO MANY

Elise Krülle opened the front door of the Witness House and almost fell to her knees in mingled alarm and respect. A middle-aged gentleman with strikingly bushy eyebrows and a narrow mustache was standing on the doorstep. Krülle immediately recognized him, for his photograph had been published many times in the local press. He was Count Roland von Faber-Castell, owner of the pen-and-pencil company. The count did not linger on the doorstep for long, but asked to speak to Rudolf Diels. For once Ingeborg Kálnoky was out of the house that morning, so Elise Krülle led the visitor into the study and asked him to wait for a moment—she would call Herr Diels down at once.

Shortly afterward the former Gestapo chief came running downstairs. Instead of staying on the first floor, however, the two men went up to Diels's room. Over the following three hours Krülle kept going into the study, because the bedroom occupied by Rudolf Diels was directly above it. The ceilings in the house were thin, and although not every word spoken upstairs could be made out, she caught a good deal of what was going on there. Elise Krülle noticed the way both men kept pacing up and down what had once been her marital bedroom, obviously deep in a very serious conversation.

Elise Krülle was sure that they could be discussing only one thing, the constant visits paid to the house in Novalisstrasse by Faber-Castell's wife, Nina. For weeks, the domestic staff of the Witness House had been busy observing and commenting on the relationship between Diels and Countess Faber-Castell. Frau Kreisel the cook had peeked around the corner when the couple was sitting in the study. Another of the domestics said he had seen them holding hands. And wasn't there a possibility that Countess Faber-Castell had even spent whole nights at the Witness House?

Countess Kálnoky kept out of these conversations. She had asked Rudolf Diels straight out what his relationship was to the lady, and she knew from her own experience how far gossip in the house could sometimes diverge from fact. Diels had told her that an old friendship of their youth linked him to Nina von Faber-Castell. He had met her in the early thirties, he said, when she was a very pretty girl of seventeen. "A gifted music student," explained Diels, "who shared with me an adventurous fondness for moving between different worlds."

During that time in Berlin, he added, she had felt a little lost, for her beloved father had recently died. Prince Friedrich Christian zu Schaumburg-Lippe, in whose spacious apartment she was staying, was a convinced supporter of the National Socialist party. From time to time the prince had acted as adjutant to Joseph Goebbels, and according to his own account of it he had met Hitler "almost daily" in the years 1933 and 1934. Later, Schaumburg-Lippe became a civil servant in the Reich Ministry of Propaganda under Goebbels—"At first, and out of pure idealism," said the prince in retrospect, explaining his commitment to the Nazis under interrogation by the U.S. prosecutor Robert Kempner, "I thought I was serving a cause which seemed to me just."

Schaumburg-Lippe had been twenty-eight in 1934, and military officers in brown Nazi uniforms went in and out of his house. They too, of course, had their eye on the prince's pretty guest. At the time Nina Sprecher von Bernegg was concentrating mainly on her music, but presumably she was also flattered by the gentlemen's advances, and she was keen to acquire experience. One day, young Nina, the daughter of a Swiss army officer, crossed the path of Rudolf Diels, and the couple fell in love.

All this was now twelve years ago. In the meantime the young music student with her lust for life had married, becoming a countess, and had given birth to three children. The youngest, Andreas, was in fact born in June 1946, in the middle of that stirring postwar period.

At the end of the war, Nina von Faber-Castell had plunged into social life as if liberated from all constraints. Since the spring of 1944 she had regularly given evening parties at the family's hunting lodge, and some of the guests, or at least Rudolf Diels and the American prosecutor Drexel Sprecher, the distant relation of Nina von Faber-Castell, were put up in her house and stayed there for days. Robert Kempner, who had presumably been introduced to the Faber-Castells by Rudolf Diels, also drove out to the hunting lodge quite frequently. The former Gestapo chief taught the countess's children the rudiments of botany, while Drexel Sprecher went trout fishing with the master of the house. In the evening Nina von Faber-Castell sat at the piano in the comfortable drawing room where a fire burned, playing songs that she had composed herself. All this time the slender, delicate young woman's pregnancy had hardly shown at all.

The baby was born on June 1, 1946, but the christening was not to be until October 20 of that year, almost four months later and several weeks after the end of the trial of the main war criminals. We can feel sure that a little party was held to celebrate the occasion. Robert Kempner and Drexel Sprecher were godfathers to the child.

Meanwhile, Ingeborg Kálnoky had her hands full at the Witness House keeping things "running smoothly" when her guests were ideologically so very different. For instance, Hitler's photographer Heinrich Hoffmann, now restored to good spirits, turned up his nose at having to share meals with a real live communist. The man's name was Franz Hemner, and he did indeed enter himself in the visitors' book in July 1946 as "representative of the Lower Rhine Communist Party of Germany." Also at the table was Erich Schwinge, a lawyer from Marburg who was later to achieve notoriety for the number of proceedings he brought against those who called him "the most feared attorney" of the Nazi period. Schwinge had written major works on the principles of National Socialist law, and as a wartime judge in Vienna had passed at least one sentence of death in a case involving a trifling offense.

Into this company came, at the beginning of August 1946, a group of former concentration camp inmates and survivors of the ghettos. There were six of them, all Jewish, "gray and slightly built," noted Ingeborg Kálnoky. Accommodating them in suitable bedrooms was no problem, but the countess was worried about her seating plan for meals. Could she seat these shadowy, enfeebled creatures next to men like Hoffmann? Kálnoky had already smoothed over many differences of opinion between her guests in the Witness House, but it seemed to her unreasonable to expect concentration camp survivors to sit next to a personal friend of Hitler. She called in Elise Krülle and asked her to help with rearranging the dining room. Instead of placing everyone around a large table, as usual, the two women now pulled the two halves of the table apart a little so that she could seat two groups of guests separately. That way, thought Kálnoky, she would have the situation under control. She was determined to "observe the utmost caution," and in no circumstances to allow any altercations.

That evening the countess ostentatiously seated herself with the new arrivals, while Hoffmann gave her a suspicious glance. Kálnoky ignored the photographer, and tried to strike up harmless "light conversation" with her new guests—she was a master of the art of communicating on trivial subjects.

However, it was not so easy to get into conversation with her new guests. Some of them spoke no German; others seemed to be reserved and deep in their own thoughts. So Ingeborg Kálnoky asked, obviously anxious to be friendly, where the men came from, and what their plans were for the immediate future. With one exception, they had spent the last few months in a camp in Munich for "displaced persons." Father Flynn had once told her that there were thousands of people in such camps, survivors of concentration camps as well as refugees from the east. Some of Kálnoky's guests were planning to emigrate to Palestine, they told her. Countess Kálnoky followed that up with a civil inquiry: "And how about your wives and children? Are they there already?"

An unbearable silence ensued, and Kálnoky could have bitten off her tongue. How could she possibly have asked such a stupid, naïve question? "I'm sorry, I didn't know . . . I mean, I didn't want to ask personal questions." She tried desperately to apologize. "I had never before come so close to the horror of it all," she said in the account she wrote in the 1940s. Suddenly, she realized, she was sitting face to face with men "whose babies had died of poison gas."

In her book written with the aid of an American ghostwriter, published in 1975 under the title *The Guest House*, she showed that she had been overwhelmed by terror when she thought of what had happened. In spite of the summer heat, she wrote in emotional tones, she shivered as if the chill of all those graves had touched her. But she obviously did not like the idea of inquiring further into what had happened to the men individually. In her first account, she does not even mention where they came from, although in the book published thirty years later she speaks of Treblinka, Majdanek, and Mauthausen. In fact the former Mauthausen concentration camp prisoners had been questioned at Nuremberg months before. Most of the men who came to the Witness House in Nuremberg in early August 1946 were Latvians or Lithuanians, and only one of them had been in the concentration camp at Majdanek. This was Israel Eisenberg, who spoke fluent German and had previously lived in Lublin.

There was an ugly scar on his left cheek. One day, on a sheer whim, some SS men in the camp had shot Eisenberg in the face. "I lay on the ground bleeding for seven hours," he said during his interrogation in Nuremberg, and only then had he finally been given medical attention. Eisenberg, an electrician, had repaired all the SS electrical equipment, first in the Lublin ghetto, later in Majdanek. In the winter of 1941 the first Jews had been deported from Lublin. "This operation involved mainly Jews who had beards," said Eisenberg in Nuremberg. "My father was one of the men taken away."

One of the men who was now sitting at that separate table in the Witness House kept throwing back his head and rolling it, "as if he had to convince himself that it was still on his shoulders," as the countess described it later in a letter. This was Leib Kibart, a leather worker, who came from the Lithuanian town of Schaulen. In the fall of 1941 about 4,500 people had been crammed into the ghetto there, and then Stormtroopers (the *Sturmabteilung*, or SA) had driven up in trucks, loaded the people into them, and shot them at a place a dozen miles away. Ghetto dwellers who tried to get hold of food had also been shot, said Kibart, testifying in court. Sometimes they died for the sake of only four or five cigarettes.

Chaim Kagan, a third member of the group of former camp inmates, had been on the Jewish Council in the ghetto of the Lithuanian town of Kovno, and told the court how approximately 10,500 Jews had been shot there in October 1941. He knew the figure, explained Kagan, because he had been the Jewish Council member responsible for catering, and a new census of the inhabitants of the ghetto had been taken after the shootings.

Szlomo Gol, who had been in the Vilna ghetto, had the most moving story of all to tell. In December 1943, he said, he and about eighty other Jews, including four women, had been picked out from the rest and placed in a pit near Vilna. SA men had put chains around their ankles and their waists, and they had had to wear these chains for six months, including the four women, who had to do kitchen work. The men's job was to dig up human corpses. "Our work consisted of opening mass graves and bringing out the bodies to be burned," said Gol in a statutory declaration made in Nuremberg. In all they had dug up eighty thousand corpses; the dead had been Jews, Polish priests, and Russian prisoners of war. Among the dead whom Gol dug out was his own brother, murdered in September 1941, who now lay in a mass grave. "I found his personal papers on him," Gol told the court.

The men stayed at the Witness House for about a week in August 1946. They had been brought to Nuremberg because their tormentors had worn the brown shirts and red swastika armbands that were the uniform of the Nazi SA. The prosecutors wanted to use the evidence of Holocaust survivors to support their case that not only the SS but also the SA were "criminal organizations." On the other hand, some of the defense lawyers tried to prove the opposite at the trial, and they too had asked witnesses to Nuremberg for that purpose: former SA functionaries or former members of the organizations incorporated into the SA—and a number of these people stayed at the Witness House under the same roof as prosecution witnesses.

These were cases of various minor Nazi functionaries: a Nazi district leader here; minor SA henchmen there, not important enough to be interned; or a leading representative of the Stahlhelm League, which had merged with the SA. In the courtroom these former SA men usually presented their organizations as some kind of sports club. For instance, there was one SA man named Dr. Menge. In a statutory declaration in court, he seriously claimed that SA Stormtroopers had protected Jewish businesses from being looted—although it could be proved that the case was exactly the opposite. This man had found a way all his own of coming to terms with the past. His entry in the visitors' book was a scribbled comment: "Difficult moments sank here into mild oblivion."

One evening an unusual conversation developed in the Witness House. Hoffmann dominated it, holding forth at length at the supper table, Kálnoky noted, "in loud and insistent tones," while the Holocaust survivors always spoke very quietly. However, this time they had taken the initiative. "Won't you tell us," one of the Jews had suddenly asked, "about your own impressions of Hitler? You can speak openly, we see this entirely objectively, without any hatred or vengeful feelings." Thereupon Heinrich Hoffmann told his Hitler anecdotes with verve, talking about his photographic art and his extraordinary experiences of taking pictures in the Berghof and the Reich Chancellery.

Ingeborg Kálnoky put these and other details into some letters that she sent in the early 1970s to the ghostwriter of her book published in 1975. During the writing of this book there was a lively correspondence between the countess and the journalist, and we can draw some interesting conclusions from it about the way the manuscript came into being. Whenever some real scene was the subject, the ghostwriter's first question was whether the participants in it were still alive—if the answer was no, she obviously felt free to invent the course of a scene for herself.

Apart from a few indications in Kálnoky's letters, there is no proof that the rest of the conversation between Hoffmann and the Holocaust survivors really took place as it is described in the ghostwriter's version. According to her, one of the survivors showed Hoffmann his wounds. This might have been Israel Eisenberg, whose scarred face could hardly be ignored. To that, we are told, Hoffmann answered brusquely that the camera is not political, and anyway he could not have photographed something when he had known absolutely nothing about it. Had he really known nothing about what was going on? asked the concentration camp inmate incredulously, or so we are told. To that Hoffmann is said to have launched into a wide-ranging speech in defense of himself and the Führer, firmly rejecting accusations of any kind of fellow traveling, let alone guilt. At least, he said, neither he nor Hitler had known anything about the concentration camps, and anyway the Führer could never have hurt a hair of anyone's head—Hitler couldn't bear the sight of blood, or so the book tells us that Hoffmann claimed.

What does seem to be confirmed by the countess's own accounts is that the Holocaust survivors listened to Hoffmann's effusions as if spellbound. Kálnoky had the impression that the photographer's stories astonished them rather than repelling them. This "humane generosity and forbearance" toward a Nazi idiot like Hoffmann deeply impressed Ingeborg Kálnoky. For a few days Hitler's photographer and the Jews were practically inseparable, the countess remembered later, shaking her head. When the Jews left, they even exchanged addresses. We do not know whether the men from Lithuania and Lublin felt any similar warmth for the SA men present. It seems unlikely, but is not entirely impossible.

It may be that the comfortable atmosphere in the villa in the Nuremberg suburbs helped to prevent any violent confrontation between the guests, however insuperable the differences between them. Presumably Ingeborg Kálnoky's charm and conversational skills simply lulled angry feelings, as if the guests were wrapped in cotton. Or perhaps no one dared to rebel out of fear of the new men in power, the Americans. Suppression of the past and self-deception on one side, with the sheer magnitude of the pain that had been suffered on the other, apparently worked to numb the minds and spirits of all concerned.

Stronger than the urge to take revenge may have been a wish to understand, in retrospect, what had happened. The more cruel and hard to grasp a crime is, the more urgent the need to understand what lies behind it can become. A rational explanation of cause and effect can give meaning to the suffering of the victims. Yet the crimes of the Nazis had been so cruel and incomprehensible that any attempt at explanation was bound to fail.

The group of Jews at the Witness House left on August 13, 1946. Only two of the six men left any trace behind in the visitors' book. Chaim Kagan, the ghetto council member from Kovno, wrote a civilly remote "Many thanks." The leather worker Leib Kibart from Schaulen even scribbled, "With warm memories." Directly below, a week later, Henriette von Schirach was to leave her mark in the form of a large-scale drawing. Her husband, Baldur von Schirach, who had been Gauleiter and Reich governor of Vienna, now on the defendants' bench, had once said of the deportation of Viennese Jews, "If anyone were to blame me for deporting tens of thousands and tens upon thousands of Jews from this city, once the European metropolis of Judaism, I must reply: I see that as an active contribution to European culture."

Henriette von Schirach went back and forth a good deal at this time, for the trial was moving more and more obviously toward the verdicts. In general she was accompanied by a crowd of American soldiers, out of either curiosity or just a preference for sensation—some of the U.S. officers obviously enjoyed being seen with Henriette, who was prominent among the Nazi women and said to have been in close contact with Hitler. The pretty woman with her thick auburn hair obviously had the same talent as her father, Heinrich Hoffmann, as Kálnoky observed, not without envy. "She could turn any situation to her own advantage."

Another relation of one of the defendants turned up at the Witness House at this time. The countess described the man as "a farmer's boy carrying a grubby old suitcase." Elmar Streicher was the son of the former Gauleiter of Franconia, Julius Streicher. The Americans had allowed him a night at the Witness House, so he gave Kálnoky a handwritten note saying, in English: "Can stay at your house for one night." It was dated September 17, 1946. Streicher was working as a farmhand, as the countess soon found out. He had come to Nuremberg to see his father one last time—for it was not at all likely that Julius Streicher would be acquitted when the verdicts, expected in the near future, were pronounced.

Ingeborg Kálnoky thought the son of the once-feared Nazi functionary was like a beaten dog. Young Streicher sat at the table that evening with his eyes lowered, and was quick to explain that politically he "did not go along" with his father's ideas.

The suspicion of being a hanger-on or of actual complicity in the criminal National Socialist system was a stigma that many people were anxious to avoid in the following years. At first imperceptibly, then more and more obviously, a sterner climate of opinion was spreading in Nuremberg. As the main trial approached its end, the prosecutors' interest in individual witnesses decreased. In line with that attitude, the Americans, who presided over the management of the Witness House, showed themselves less and less willing to make concessions. Some of the witnesses suddenly had to move to an internment camp; others continued to be officially classified as POWs and were simply forgotten; still others unexpectedly found themselves at liberty, only to be swiftly arrested again.

That was the case with Paul Otto Schmidt, former interpreter in chief to the German Foreign Office. A diplomat who, as Hitler's personal interpreter, had taken part in almost all the Führer's meetings with foreign heads of government, he had ended as manager of Foreign Minister Ribbentrop's office. The Americans kept him in prison for months after the end of the war, and he gave evidence against Ribbentrop several times at the main trial. Finally, in the fall of 1946, Robert Kempner got him out of prison and had him transferred to the Witness House, where it seems that Countess Kálnoky found she could listen for hours on end to the astute little man with the high, bald forehead while he told stories from his eventful life in the diplomatic service—he had served under the now-legendary foreign minister Gustav Stresemann during the Weimar Republic period.

However, a few months after he had moved into the Witness House, he was suddenly removed from it again. The prosecutors suspected Paul Otto Schmidt, in his capacity as Ribbentrop's office manager, of having been involved in a plot to murder a French general. The charge could not be substantiated, but once again Schmidt was held for a considerable time in the prisoners' wing of the courthouse building. It was to be Robert Kempner who extricated him once more, many months later, although not as an act of charity. Kempner wanted Schmidt as a witness for the prosecution in the subsequent trial of Foreign Ministry officials, which was to begin in 1947.

In the fall of 1946, even Rudolf Diels had to leave the hospitable Witness House temporarily. He wrote his name in the visitors' book, but no more. Where exactly he was transferred is not clear, but he could not go home, so he was faced with a delicate problem. Shortly before he left, Diels asked the countess to come up to his room; she must, absolutely must, do him another favor, he said. He brought out a case containing a pink negligee, a dreamy creation of tulle and silk. It belonged to Countess Faber-Castell, and Diels was looking for a way to get it back to its rightful owner as discreetly as possible. If he didn't, he told Kálnoky, the consequences would be terrible.

Ingeborg Kálnoky gave the former Gestapo chief an ironic glance. Hadn't he spun her a yarn about an innocent youthful friendship? But then she called in the aid of Elise Krülle and asked her to see to it. A little later, Krülle's niece Elisabeth Kühnle set out with the little case, which was returned to its owner's hands without any further incident. Elisabeth Kühnle, however, was never to forget this little episode. The negligee, she said, was "as beautiful as a ball dress." By way of thanks she was given a vacation at a spa resort for herself and her baby—Countess Faber-Castell had obviously exerted influence on the local representative of the new mothers' convalescent home organization.

Generalmajor Ulrich Keßler von der deutschen Luftwaffe ist mit seinem Stab und anderen hohen Offizieren erst fünf Tage nach dem Waffenstillstand von den Amerikanern auf einem U-Boot gefangen genommen worden. Auf der Ueberfahrt nach U.S.A. kann er sich die Zeit mit einem Buch vertreiben, das sich mit den Nachkriegsproblemen beschäftigt,

General Erwin Lahousen, star prosecution witness in Nuremberg. Countess Kálnoky kept this newspaper photograph for many years.

A prominent general in the Witness House: the Luftwaffe commander Ulrich Kessler, also from a press cutting that was in the Countess's possession.

The most athletic of the generals: Ernst Köstring, whose last posting was as military attaché to Moscow, went jogging in the garden of the Witness House. Heinrich Hoffmann photographed him at the supper table in the villa.

The Kálnoky children: Fárkas, Lori, Antal, and Ingeborg, after the family's move to the USA in 1949.

They married in Thuringia in 1934: Hugo Count Kálnoky and his bride Ingeborg von Breitenbuch.

A dream castle in Transylvania: Köröspatak, residence of the Kálnokys. At the end of the 1930s the Hungarian family had to leave their property, under pressure from the Romanian government.

Beginning again was difficult after her arrival in America: Countess Kálnoky in the 1950s.

The Krülles, father and son, outside their new house at the end of the 1930s—who would have thought that one day witnesses at a war crimes trial would stay there?

Family idyll before the outbreak of war: Walter Krülle volunteered to go to the front, and never came home.

A witness in Nuremberg: Auschwitz survivor Marie-Claude Vaillant-Couturier, photographed by the Spaniard Franceso Boix, gave evidence about the Mauthausen camp at the main trial.

Debilitated and starving: prisoners in the Buchenwald concentration camp on April 16, 1945, the day of their liberation by the Americans.

In the Mauthausen concentration camp on May 6, 1945: Spanish prisoners put up a banner on the camp wall to greet their liberators.

An aircraft constructor who stood in high favor with the Nazis: Willy Messerschmitt (right) in conversation with Hermann Göring in 1941.

In diese harten Zeit, in der Neid, Haß und Mißgunst die Gehirne der Menschheit leiten und Güte so selten geworden ist, danke ich Ihnen, verehrte Baronin, die Sie die Pflichten der Hausfrau für dieses Haus übernommen haben, für die sorgende Pflege, die ich so warm empfunden habe.

Willy Messerschmitt

20.2.47.

Messerschmitt's entry in the second visitors' book of the Witness House, February 1947.

In the Witness House at the same time: Josef Ackermann, former prisoner in Dora-Mittelbau camp, where Messerschmitt aircraft parts were assembled.

A cross-examination like a battle: the writer Eugen Kogon was violently attacked by the defense counsel at Nuremberg in 1947.

A Resistance fighter who met managers of the Flick industrial company at the Witness House: Robert Havemann.

The minutes of the Wannsee Conference. Only this one copy, out of thirty, was ever found, and then not until 1947, after the end of the main trial.

Fabian Flynn, Catholic priest, a U.S. army chaplain, and a frequent visitor to the Witness House.

Universally admired, and often envied: Ingeborg Countess Kálnoky at the Witness House, photo taken in 1946 by Hitler's personal photographer, Heinrich Hoffmann.

She kept her souvenirs of Nuremberg all her life: Countess Kálnoky in 1995, in her apartment in Cleveland, with her old visitors' book from Novalisstrasse.

After the war, he worked as a lawyer for the cause of those persecuted by the Nazis: Robert Kempner in 1969, in his legal office in Frankfurt.

WILLY MESSERSCHMITT
AND MATHEMATICS

There had been a vague tension in the air for days. Gerhard Krülle felt the suspense almost physically. When he came home from school that Tuesday, he could already hear a loud voice over the radio as he reached the stairwell of the Witness House. The broadcast seemed to be coming from the second floor, where a group of guests had gathered in a small room. Normally the boy never ventured into it; they were in Countess Kálnoky's bedroom. But now he made his way through the door and joined the others in the room.

The court had reached its verdicts in the first, main trial of war criminals, and the radio announcer was just beginning to read out the sentences passed on the individual defendants. Death sentence followed death sentence. They were all listening to the broadcast with bated breath. Gerhard Krülle looked around the room. He saw the photographer Hoffmann sitting on Kálnoky's bed, with his wife and his daughter, Henriette. Henriette's hands were in constant movement. Ambassador Rintelen, who had spent last winter immersed in *Meyer's Encyclopedia*, was back again. He kept his distance, as haughty as ever. Ten or twelve people in all were crammed into the small room, and the countess sat enthroned in the middle, concentrating entirely on the sentences as they were read out.

When the radio announcer reached the name of Baldur von Schirach, a sharp cry broke the silence in the little room. Schirach had been condemned not to death but to twenty years' imprisonment. His wife, Henriette, was visibly relieved; "He will live!" The next moment the voice on the radio was announcing that Albert Speer, Hitler's architect and minister of war, was to receive the same sentence of twenty years. Henriette abruptly stood up and, with her parents, went to the photographer's room on the other side of the corridor. The Hoffmanns wanted to celebrate their pleasure at the leniency of the sentence in private. When Henriette von Schirach was called later to the telephone in the stairwell, her happy voice filled the whole house. "Isn't that wonderful? Now he'll have twenty years to play chess with Albert Speer."

With the reading of the sentences early in the afternoon of October 1, 1946, the main trial of the most prominent war criminals came to an end. Twelve defendants had been condemned to death by hanging, among them: Hermann Göring; former foreign minister Ribbentrop; the Nazi governor-general of Poland Hans Frank; the former Reich minister of labor Fritz Sauckel; and Julius Streicher, Gauleiter of Franconia. As well as Schirach and Speer, five other defendants had been given jail sentences ranging from ten years to life. Three of the accused were acquitted: Hjalmar Schacht, the former head of the Reich Bank; Franz von Papen, formerly Reich chancellor; and Hans Fritzsche, for many years the chief press officer of the National Socialist government.

In the middle of October 1946, Kálnoky's contact officer told her to expect a new guest at the Witness House, a Dr. Schmidt. This gentleman was driven up in a large limousine by a high-ranking American officer. He was in his mid-sixties and very well dressed, as the countess noticed. The atmosphere was muted that evening of October 15. Everyone present knew that the death sentences were to be carried out that night. Dr. Schmidt appeared reserved. Hoffmann tried laboriously to get a conversation going with him. "You're from Munich?" he said, pursuing this line in his usual jovial way. "We must have met there, I'm sure." Schmidt did not react. Hoffmann thought for a moment. Then he made another attempt to get the new-comer talking. "Are you by any chance *the* Dr. Schmidt, the well-known fashionable physician?" The stranger said he was not, and the conversation died down yet again. Hoffmann pulled out all the stops trying to get the man talking, but to no avail. After the meal, Dr. Schmidt excused himself, saying that he had another appointment.

The silent Dr. Schmidt did not come back at all that eve-ning. Feeling anxious about him, Ingeborg Kálnoky informed the courthouse officer, but he did not pay any particular atten-tion to the news. When she picked up a newspaper the next day she realized who the mysterious stranger must have been: the minister president of Bavaria, Wilhelm Hoegner, a Social Democrat who had been living in exile during the National Socialist period. Hoegner had been present at the executions as a "representative of the German people." News of the execu-tions themselves was overshadowed by the report that Göring had accelerated his own death by committing suicide. Around the table in the Witness House that evening there was excited speculation: how on earth had the old fox managed to keep a cyanide capsule concealed on his person?

A few days later, a German police car drove into Novalis-strasse. Two plainclothes officers got out and walked briskly up to the Witness House—they had come for Heinrich Hoff-mann. They were soon explaining to the startled photographer that from now on he was under their protection, and that they would not leave his side by day or night. The police officers accompanied Hoffmann to court and went to the Golden Star inn with him. At night one of them took up his post outside Hoffmann's door, while the other slept in the next room. Hoffmann didn't let this attention spoil his good humor. The Americans had asked him to find somewhere private to stay after the end of the trial, he told the countess, and the policemen had been given the job of protecting him until he had found a permanent place to live, "because I haven't been denazified yet."

Denazification—in Hoffmann's mouth, it sounded like no more than an unwelcome visit to the dentist. In fact it amounted to something like a legal process, carried out in "denazification courts," before which people had to appear if they had been Party members during the National Socialist period, or had drawn attention to themselves in any way as supporters of the regime. Lay judges in the denazification courts graded those affected into five categories according to their degree of involvement, ranging from the definitely guilty to hangers-on to individuals who could be exonerated entirely. Many of these proceedings were opened only after a delay of years; others were never opened. In the case of Heinrich Hoffmann the presiding lay judge of the local denazification committee soon turned up in person at the Witness House, as the countess remembered, and had the photographer arrested. Two police officers took him to their car, like a criminal, with Hoffmann's wife in pursuit calling them names. Erna Hoffmann, who had always boasted of her husband's good relationship with the Führer, seemed to have no guilty conscience at all about the Nazi period. When the police car drove away she was left behind in the street, infuriated. "Are they never going to leave us in peace?" she cried.

The trial of the main war criminals, conducted in the glaring light of international publicity, was over. But the American prosecution had already begun preparing for the first trials that were to follow.* New guests arrived at the Witness House, summoned to Nuremberg for questioning: managers of the IG Farben company, directors of the Krupp steelworks. Rudolf Diels had also returned to Novalisstrasse, and Ambassador Rintelen was to stay for a few more weeks. Finally, the aircraft designer and builder Willy Messerschmitt arrived one day. He had already spent several months in internment, had been flown to England during that time, and had been arrested and freed again several times. Originally the Americans wanted to take him to the States, where other leading German scientists were already at work on research into atomic fission and space flight. But Messerschmitt had said he would go to the United States only as a private person, not as a scientist.

Soon before the verdict in the main trial the Americans had summoned him to Nuremberg and initially put him in the prison wing of the courthouse building. In his first interrogations, Messerschmitt, whom Hitler had once made "leader of defense in industry," protested that he was prone to melancholy and had therefore suffered from depression after his recent arrests. After a few weeks the prosecutors showed leniency, and Messerschmitt was allowed to move to the Witness House in November 1946. He was soon asking the countess for a drawing board, paper, compasses, a ruler, and pencils. "I suppose he couldn't live without dreaming up technical innovations," she commented.

Drawing implements were found for him, and soon the aircraft constructor was seen working on new inventions. His technical drawings were done in fine, thin lines, like spiderwebs stretching over his sketchpad. "He was going to invent

---

* There were twelve of these secondary trials in all.

a vacuum cleaner," the countess said later. "He asked if we already had an electrical sweeper, and wondered whether an entirely new kind of bed might not be constructed."

The old lady sat enthroned in her little apartment in Cleveland, Ohio, in her armchair as usual, as she told me about Willy Messerschmitt. Outside, thick snowflakes were still falling silently to the ground; inside, the TV screen was flickering again. Ingeborg Kálnoky shook her head over the aircraft designer, smiling. "Whatever was inside that forehead of his, it must have been different from other people's brains," she surmised. "He had a technician's brain, pure and simple."

In the evening, the professor gave lectures on space flight at the Witness House. In the morning, the Americans questioned him in the courthouse building about the development of Hitler's V-2 miracle weapon, a long-distance rocket that was shrouded in mystery. They asked what he knew about the background armaments activities of the Nazis, and tried to gain some insight into the baffling circumstances surrounding the ownership of his aircraft firms. In the afternoons, out of sheer boredom, Willy Messerschmitt sometimes helped young Gerhard Krülle with his math homework. "He had told my mother, if your boy has any difficulties I'd be happy to help him," Professor Krülle told me later.

One day—Gerhard was now fourteen and going to high school—the boy really was unable to solve some particularly difficult problems. Messerschmitt sat down to look at them, calculated and calculated, and scribbled two pages of Gerhard's exercise book full of figures. However, the end result was "$0 = 0$." "Messerschmitt couldn't make head or tail of it either," Krülle told me, still as happy as a schoolboy about the incident decades later. Krülle kept the two pages on which Messerschmitt had written his calculations for a long time. The boy's encounters with Messerschmitt must have made a great impression on him, for later Gerhard Krülle himself specialized in research into space flight.

Life at the Witness House continued on an even keel. During the day, Ingeborg Kálnoky often stood at her easel, painting. She even asked Willy Messerschmitt to sit for his portrait, so the good-natured aircraft constructor patiently sat on a chair while she sketched his features. Sadly, the finished portrait has not been preserved. In the evenings Kálnoky sat at the typewriter that Father Flynn had given her. She described recent events and worked on her account of the Witness House. Meanwhile, down in the study, it was harder and harder for her to get an entertaining conversation going. Heinrich Hoffmann's son had come to Nuremberg on his father's behalf, and stayed at the Witness House. He represented the interests of his father's archive in court. From the countess's point of view, this new guest was not a sociable addition to the company. She gained an increasing impression that the days of the Witness House in its prime were over—"suddenly we were not the right kind of arrangement anymore."

While those well established at the Witness House still enjoyed lavish provisions supplied by the Americans in the old way, in the outside world the young democracy was taking shape. Even at over seventy, Carl Severing, the Social Democrat, was working on the country's political reconstruction. Severing became involved in the Social Democratic Party (SPD) election campaign, and sent the countess pages of single-spaced, typed letters that read like political manifestos. Ingeborg Kálnoky probably never read any of them very closely.

The winter of 1946/47 was particularly long and cold, and the people of Germany suffered more extreme hunger than ever. In Nuremberg a large portion of the population was still living in ruins or cellars. More and more refugees from the east were arriving all the time, and the number of displaced and homeless people who had no roof over their heads had risen drastically. Some of the homeless had to stay in those camps into which, during the war, the Jews had been crammed before deportation. Father Flynn had told Kálnoky about the suffering of the people in camps for the homeless. "A can of milk is like a gold bar there," was one of his remarks about the situation.

The priest seemed to be driven by a constant need to be where the misery was at its worst. Without a doubt, food shortages were among the most urgent problems in Germany, so Flynn had recently left his army service and become involved in a huge Catholic aid organization, the War Relief Services of the National Catholic Welfare Conference. It is not clear exactly when he began working for this organization. In mid-October 1946 he was still in Nuremberg, and according to a report in the *Notiziario Passionista*, an Italian-language information publication of his order, he attended the executions as a priest. In January 1947, according to a note in the *Passionist Bulletin*, Flynn was already working in Freiburg im Breisgau, and went on from there to take charge of the Catholic aid organizations in the zone of French occupation. Previously he may well have visited the countess once more, and contact between them probably continued.

On one of the last days of January 1947, Elise Krülle opened the door of the Witness House to a gentleman entirely unknown to her, wearing what looked like a foreign uniform. It was Hugo Count Kálnoky, the countess's husband, who had been missing for so long. His two eldest children, Lori and Fárkas, recognized him at once. Fárkas particularly admired his fine uniform, which had more gold lace on it than he had seen any of the officers in Nuremberg wearing. At first their younger

brother, Antal, seemed to think he was a new witness, as Kálnoky later remembered, and Bobbie, who was now nearly one
and a half, had never seen her father before. The countess herself was overwhelmed. She had heard nothing from her husband for nearly two years, and now, all of a sudden, here he
was, and everything seemed to be back to normal. But was it
really?

Hugo Count Kálnoky had returned as a representative of
the Red Cross, hence the fine uniform. But his face was pale
and his stomach looked unhealthily bloated. For the last two
years he had lived almost entirely on beans. He had done the
heaviest of forced labor every day, because the Soviets could
tell from his hands that he was not by birth a manual laborer.
However, Hugo Kálnoky had succeeded in hiding his aristocratic origins from the new regime in power in Eastern Europe.
He had made contact with the Red Cross as soon as he could
to find out where his family was, but without success. One day
a Red Cross delegation was to be sent to the West to negoti-
ate the return of various Hungarian possessions now outside
the country. Someone remembered that Hugo Kálnoky could
speak several languages, and he was chosen to accompany the
delegation.

Only on reaching Germany was the count able to find out
where his wife was living. He had no idea that she was managing a guesthouse in Nuremberg. Not only, therefore, was the
countess surprised to see *him*, her husband too was unprepared
to find her doing such a job. His wife had clearly changed. She
was no longer the mistress of Köröspatak before whom the servants used to kneel in respect on feast days, kissing her hands,
and who was accustomed to having all kinds of attentions lav-
ished on her by her husband. Kálnoky had learned to stand on
her own feet, and the landed aristocratic lady had adjusted to

middle-class life. However, her husband obviously felt the same almost chivalrous duty to look after her. He wanted to build a new castle suitable for his beloved wife as soon as he could.

Admittedly the count lacked funds for anything like that in Nuremberg, but he hoped to find a firm footing quickly in Austria, where he had been born and had relations. Ingeborg Kálnoky went along with his wishes and gave notice that she was leaving her post, and a few days after her husband's arrival the whole family traveled to Austria. In her baggage the countess had an excellent reference, written on January 30, 1947, testifying to her time at the Witness House. In this document the officer in charge of the villa, Major Thomas K. Hodges of the military administration's personnel office, praised the "superior manner" in which Kálnoky had "mastered a difficult task in connection with the International Military Tribunal." In her position as manager of the Witness House, he said, tact and infallible judgment had been needed, and the countess had left nothing to be desired in that respect.

When Kálnoky suddenly gave notice, the Americans were obliged to find a replacement for her very quickly—and once again they engaged an aristocrat. Annemarie von Kleist probably took over the management of the Witness House on February 1, 1947. Her husband, Bernhard von Kleist, who was working as an interpreter for the Americans, may have found the position for her.

Bernhard von Kleist was forty-four years old at the time, and already had an eventful career behind him. As a young man he had fought in one of the reactionary Freikorps* organizations,

---

* The Freikorps were private freelance fighting units, formed when the Treaty of Versailles strictly limited the size of the German army after the First World War. Their members, right-wing militants, were exactly the kind of men that Hitler subsequently recruited into the SS.

whose members had shot down rebellious workers in the Ruhr in the early twenties. In 1921 he went to Morocco and trained as a businessman, and in 1924 he married a Spanish woman, Julia López de Uruburu. Three years later the couple went to live first in Venezuela and then in Colombia, where Kleist worked in civil engineering, building highways and railroads.

All was well with them for several years, until Bernhard von Kleist contracted malaria. He went first to Canada, and finally, in 1933, returned to Europe, where he leased a farm near Riga and tried his hand at agriculture. His Spanish wife does not seem to have liked the rugged north, and in 1934 the couple divorced. Soon after that, Kleist married Annemarie Neumann, the daughter of a chemist from Dorpat in Estonia.

In the Witness House the new manager, though born a middle-class girl, soon appeared as the perfect baroness—Elise Krülle and her son Gerhard, at least, thought she was over-doing the aristocratic airs and graces. Presumably the shrewd Elise had a good idea that the Kleists must in fact be extremely glad to have found such a pleasant place to live as the villa in Novalisstrasse. Bernhard von Kleist had worked initially as an interpreter and language teacher in a camp for displaced persons in Bayreuth, where he and his wife seem to have found themselves almost by chance after the turbulent days of the war. Kleist, as a farmer, had not been called up to go to the front until the last year of the war, and once there he suffered a bad leg wound that was to remain a disability for the rest of his life.

The Kleists probably did not arrive in Nuremberg until near the end of the main trial, when extra interpreters were being sought for the secondary trials. It was a great piece of luck for the family that while Bernhard found a good post as a court interpreter, so did Annemarie as manager of the Witness House.

The couple and their two children moved into Novalisstrasse, and from then on Annemarie von Kleist ran the house.

Of course Baroness von Kleist also kept a visitors' book. This was the second book, the one that Bernhard von Kleist had shown us at my parents' house, the Bear Mill, on the evening of August 31, 1980. Bound in brown leather, adorned with a thin line of gold leaf, the album has been preserved to this day, although the gilt on the cut edges of the paper has yellowed slightly now, and the cover of the book is coming a bit loose.

The first guest to write his name in it, on February 5, 1947, was a director of the IG Farben company named Anton Reithinger. The chemical company's manager had obviously come to the Witness House before, weeks earlier, for he praised the introduction of an afternoon coffee hour as "the most important initiative of the new management." In addition Reithinger recommended that every new guest bring cards for playing bridge, "and the lady of the house will be grateful to him."

During this time, all was not quite so innocent and neutral in the Witness House as the industrialist's entry might suggest. The first phase of the trials indeed ended with the verdicts on the principal war criminals. However, the subsequent trials contained what was, fundamentally, material of potentially explosive importance for postwar German society, concentrating as they did on questions of guilt and expiation. Some of these investigations, for instance, were concerned with the part played by doctors or lawyers in the murder and persecution of the innocent. These cases examined the actual complicity of certain government civil servants, the involvement of large industries such as IG Farben and Krupp in the Holocaust, and the exploitation of forced labor.

Once again, the guilty and their victims were to come closer to each other in the Witness House than anywhere else in Germany.

A PRISONER'S PACT WITH THE DEVIL

The woman seemed shy, she did not talk much, and somehow she gave the impression that her spirit was broken. Annemarie von Kleist instantly felt that this slender, pale woman could only be a former prisoner, and so she wrote "concentration camp witness" in pencil in the margin when the guest left her name in the visitors' book in March 1947. Gisa Punzengruber had in fact worked in a hospital, never setting foot in a concentration camp. However, during her stay at the Witness House, Punzengruber, who was twenty-eight at the time, was to see her private life collapse like a house of cards—and that was indeed to do with the Dachau concentration camp.

She worked as a medical technical assistant, or MTA, in a laboratory attached to the Munich hospital described as "Links der Isar" (Left of the river Isar). During the war she had met Rudolf Punzengruber there. He was a qualified doctor of chemistry who, from 1942 onward, regularly came to the hospital to collect medicines and chemicals and was always accompanied by an SS man. After a while Punzengruber told her that he was an inmate of a concentration camp, and the two became friends. They married after the war, in October 1945. But Rudolf's visits to the hospital had always been shrouded in mystery. "Don't ask me what I do or where I come from," the chemist had told his future wife again and again. It was

probably not until she was in Nuremberg that Gisa Punzengruber first understood the full extent of the horrors that her
husband had tried to conceal from her behind such vague hints.
The chemist, born in Carinthia, Austria, in 1900, had started
his professional life managing a mine in Serbia. In 1941, now a
Yugoslavian citizen, he was arrested, presumably for insufficient
conformity to National Socialist principles. Rudolf Punzengruber was interned first in Vienna, then in the Dachau concentration camp. There he met Sigmund Rascher, an SS doctor who
used concentration camp prisoners for medical experiments.
Rascher would, for instance, carry out experiments on freezing
on behalf of the Luftwaffe. The subjects of these experiments
were forcibly exposed to temperatures below freezing that
would inevitably be fatal to the human organism. The scientists
were testing, on living people, how long a human being could
stand up to such exposure before perishing in agony.

Punzengruber became Rascher's assistant, and he obviously
did his work so much to the SS doctor's satisfaction that in the
fall of 1943 Rascher supported a request for Punzengruber to
be freed, although on the condition that the chemist continue
to help him voluntarily with his experiments. This was what
must have been a very rare instance of a concentration camp
prisoner who became an active member of the Waffen SS. The
head of the SS, Heinrich Himmler, who was on friendly terms
with Rascher, had evidently arranged personally for Punzengruber to join the SS.

The Rascher case had already been mentioned in the course
of the main trial of the principal war criminals in Nuremberg.
The SS doctor was regarded as one of the most appalling instances of the way a medical career could be perverted under
the Third Reich. When the Doctors' Trial began, around the
turn of the year from 1946 to 1947, the American prosecutors

brought up the Rascher case again. At this point the SS doctor himself had been dead for some time, but the prosecutors aimed to bring his superiors and colleagues to justice. For that reason, not only was Gisa Punzengruber brought to Nuremberg, but also Fritz Rascher, the father of the accused doctor—and they were both staying at the Witness House.

Rascher senior had arrived in December 1946, when Countess Kálnoky was still in Novalisstrasse. Subsequently he was questioned by various prosecuting teams, and he also appeared as a witness at the Doctors' Trial that began early that December. Presumably Fritz Rascher stayed at the Witness House for several weeks. Gisa Punzengruber was in Nuremberg in January and March 1947—so her stay in Novalisstrasse would have coincided with the older Rascher's for at least a short time. Very likely the doctor, who had a homeopathic practice in Munich, still did not realize just what his son Sigmund had been capable of doing. He had brought him up on liberal principles and sent him to one of the Waldorf schools following the educational tenets of Rudolf Steiner. Even as a child, however, Rascher junior had once modeled a figure that "deeply disturbed" his father, now sixty-six years old, as he told his interrogator in Nuremberg. It was as if the devil himself looked out of that figure, said Fritz Rascher.

The SS doctor Sigmund Rascher later had many people murdered in Dachau, sometimes personally giving them an injection of prussic acid, "purely for his private entertainment," as Rudolf Punzengruber said. However, the Americans soon realized that the chemist himself was deeply involved in Rascher's machinations. For the price of his freedom, Punzengruber had made a pact with the devil.

The pact obviously went so far that he himself had plumbed the depths of the SS doctor's mind. Sigmund Rascher had been killed in 1944 on Himmler's orders, not in retribution for any professional misdemeanor but for his private transgressions. Since the Raschers could not have children of their own, Rascher's wife—apparently a former mistress of Himmler—had stolen several children. The deception had come to light one day when Frau Rascher was in an air raid shelter and was denounced by others seeking refuge there. Thereupon the SS doctor and his wife were both arrested, and eliminated soon after.

After the liberation of Dachau, the Americans had arrested Rudolf Punzengruber on information provided by other prisoners in the camp. From then on Punzengruber had enough to say about the SS doctor to fill volumes, while always trying to hush up his own role. The chemist had been interned yet again in Dachau, but was presumably moved to the prison wing of the Nuremberg courthouse while interrogations went on. Obviously the Americans considered Rudolf Punzengruber so guilty that only his frail physical constitution kept him from joining the defendants in the Doctors' Trial. The questioning of the witness Punzengruber in February 1947 brought to light, bit by bit, details of the extent of his collaboration with Dr. Sigmund Rascher. However, his wife, Gisa Punzengruber, claimed to have "known nothing at all" about it. She protested: "He always refused to tell me anything."

Irene Seiler was also in Nuremberg at about the same time as Gisa Punzengruber. A professional photographer, thirty-six years old, Seiler had spent almost two years in prison during the war. Now, at the Witness House, she met one of the judges who had passed sentence on her in 1942. Hugo Hoffmann was a narrow-shouldered man with glasses and a neat side part in his hair—the photographer almost failed to recognize him in Novalisstrasse. Only when someone pointed him out to her did she look at him more closely.

In 1942 Hoffmann and two other judges had condemned the president of the Jewish religious community in Nuremberg, Leo Katzenberger, to death for allegedly breaking the race laws forbidding sexual relationships between Jews and non-Jews. His fellow defendant, Irene Seiler, was to serve a sentence of two years in prison for her part in the crime. Katzenberger, who had been sixty-eight at the time, was accused of "immoral relations" with the photographer. Irene Seiler was found guilty of perjury because she had refused to confess to intimacies forbidden by the Nazis under what was called the Law for the Protection of German Blood. There was no evidence for the couple's alleged transgressions, but nonetheless Katzenberger was executed in Stadelheim Prison, Munich, in June 1942. Meanwhile Irene Seiler was first sent to Aichach prison, then set to work in a munitions factory filling ammunition cases with explosives. The yellowish powder ate into her skin and hair.

And now, five years after this textbook example of autocratic Nazi justice, Irene Seiler found herself staying in the comfortable middle-class surroundings of number 24 Novalisstrasse, Nuremberg, with one of her former tormentors. Hoffmann made haste to denounce the verdict in Katzenberger's case at that time as "intolerable, unjust, and inhuman." The presiding judge at Katzenberger's trial, Oswald Rothaug, was now on the defendants' bench in the Judges' Trial, the third of the subsidiary American military tribunals. Hoffmann, who was in Nuremberg as a witness, did not believe that he bore any of the responsibility himself: "Rothaug was to blame for it all," he explained. "We were only unimportant little court associates, we couldn't have done anything wrong."

From his own point of view as "only a court associate," the National Socialist judge Hoffmann held that he had almost nothing to do with the passing of that death sentence, and about a dozen others in which, on his own admission, he could be shown to have played a part. But Irene Seiler, also in Nuremberg as a witness in the Judges' Trial, was cross-examined by Rothaug's defense counsel in such a way that she was bound to feel almost as if she were the defendant again. She returned to the Witness House downcast after her questioning, and her entry in the visitors' book when she left was a simple proverbial truism: "Sunshine will follow the rain." Judge Hoffmann, on the other hand, wrote a fulsome rhyming tribute in the book, to the effect that while, as the Nazi judge saw it, "elsewhere witch hunts do abound," at the Witness House "a human haven may be found."

What can the feelings of Robert Havemann have been when he stayed at the Witness House? The Resistance worker had to sit at the table with a manager from the Flick company, a firm that had enriched itself lavishly from the labor of concentration camp inmates. Havemann himself had spent just under two years in the Brandenburg penitentiary. He had been condemned to death for high treason in 1944 after a small Resistance group in Berlin going by the name of "European Union" was uncovered; he and a handful of like-minded people had founded it. In prison Havemann, a highly qualified chemist who was to be distinguished as a professor in his subject later, managed to convince the Nazis that before his arrest he had been working on research important to the war effort. He was then sent to a laboratory in Brandenburg, and for that reason alone the execution of his death sentence was repeatedly postponed, so that in the end Havemann survived.

The chemist was in Nuremberg, like Hoffmann and Seiler, to give evidence in the Judges' Trial. Presumably Berthold Schwarz was staying at the Witness House at the same time. Schwarz was a trained lawyer and a former SS man who had been a specialist in cases of high treason, and finally adviser on clemency in the central prosecutors' office of the High Court of the Reich—in this capacity, he may have been familiar with Havemann's file. In the courtroom Schwarz gave evidence directly after the Resistance man. His entry in the visitors' book is dated a little earlier than Havemann's, but the lawyer had been in Nuremberg twice, and apparently left an entry in the book only after his first visit.

Usually those who left a record of themselves in this album were representatives of the fallen National Socialist regime. Resistance members and victims of the Nazis, on the other hand, either wrote no entry or left only a very brief one. Robert Havemann was the only one of these victims to write more than three words in either of the two visitors' books. "Nuremberg—a world in ruins, and its ghosts are conjured up here," the chemist wrote on April 11, 1947. "We will not forget that world, we will overcome it."

At meals in Novalisstrasse there were sometimes unpleasant surprises for individual guests. The Munich journalist Josef Ackermann, for instance, found himself sitting between supporters of the old regime who, he thought, would have been behind bars by this time. Ackermann's neighbor at the dining table was Friedrich Gaus, formerly a leading company lawyer in the Foreign Office. As a diplomat, this man had formulated almost all the international agreements of Hitler's government. Diagonally opposite the journalist sat a director of the Krupp works who said that he really had not taken any notice of the slave laborers employed in the armaments firm—and so, in conversation with Ackermann, he also denied feeling any kind of responsibility.

A little later that evening Rudolf Diels joined the company. By now he was no longer under house arrest, he could move around Nuremberg almost as he liked, and he had taken up residence at the Witness House again. Ackermann remembered only too well that Diels had been head of the Gestapo at the time when he first found himself in Dachau.

The journalist, who was to become press officer for the city of Munich after the war, had spent almost the whole Nazi period in camps and prisons. He was first arrested in September 1933 for treason, accused of writing in disparaging terms about the new Nazi government for British newspapers. For this offense both he and the correspondent of the London *Daily News* were arrested. Ackermann spent a year in Dachau, until fall 1934. At that time people were being beaten to death in the concentration camp for no reason at all. In the years 1935 to 1939 the journalist was arrested again and again, and he became all too familiar with the notorious Gestapo prison in the Wittelsbach Palace in Munich.

In September 1939, the Gestapo arrested him once more, and this time Ackermann was not even given any reason. A few days later he was transferred to the Buchenwald concentration camp, and from then on the journalist was to stay behind barbed wire until the end of the war. First he spent three and a half years in Buchenwald, where he had to keep a record of deaths in the pathology department. Ackermann saw all kinds of things in the camp, such as the way gold teeth were carefully removed from the dead—"They were handed over in a bag to the head of administration," said the journalist at Nuremberg.

While Ackermann was in Buchenwald the camp doctor there was writing a doctoral dissertation on tattooing. For purposes of his own research, he collected large quantities of human skin. The patches of skin bearing tattoos were exhibited in little boxes, like a butterfly collection. Ackermann gave evidence that murder was arbitrarily committed in Buchenwald for the sake of getting fine tattoos and heads that could be successfully shrunk. The camp doctor might stand at a window and point to a certain inmate, said the Munich journalist during his questioning in Nuremberg. "I'd like his head in my collection," the doctor would comment—"And next day that prisoner was on the dissection table," said Ackermann.

Early in 1944 the journalist was moved to the Dora-Mittelbau concentration camp, situated underground in a long range of hills on the southern outskirts of the Harz Mountains near Nordhausen. Hitler had the prisoners put to work in the subterranean tunnels and galleries, building what was supposed to be his miracle weapon, the "Vergeltungswaffe 2" (Retaliation Weapon 2), V-2 for short: a long-distance rocket that could break the sound barrier. In addition, the exhausted concentration camp inmates had to assemble aircraft parts for Luftwaffe planes. Among these were engines for one of the jet fighters designed by Willy Messerschmitt, series name Me 262. Messerschmitt affectionately called this plane his "swallow" because of its good qualities in flight. Ackermann could reel off the names of many prisoners who had died in the cruel labor conditions while assembling airplane parts. The meeting of the two men at the Witness House in the spring of 1947 looked like a heartless parlor game played by fate.

Messerschmitt, like Diels, was slightly late for supper that evening, and the company was already on the dessert course when they came in. Ackermann, who recognized the aircraft constructor at once, almost dropped his spoon. Messerschmitt, however, presumably did not even guess that he was sitting opposite a former inmate of Dora-Mittelbau. The Americans had asked him about the concentration camp several times, but the aircraft constructor always claimed that he "couldn't really remember" certain details.

However, Willy Messerschmitt had been in the tunnels of Dora-Mittelbau at least once, in March 1945. At this time Josef Ackermann was working in the sick bay of the camp. Closely questioned by the Americans, Messerschmitt could remember the railroad tracks leading to the galleries, and he spoke of the underground tunnels that were broad enough for two freight trains to pass through them at the same time. He also described the small stairway leading up to the works office—the green huts where a large number of the camp inmates were quartered, and the tall wire fence that surrounded the entire area but which, previously, he said he had not seen.

Inside the tunnels too, the former managing director of Bavarian Aircraft Works claimed not to have noticed anything in particular. Had he been aware, asked one of the prosecutors, that Dora was kept running "mainly by exploiting the labor of concentration camp inmates?" No, replied Messerschmitt. "But it was practically impossible to overlook the fact," said the U.S. officer questioning him, and he added, "Who *did* you see doing the work, then?" Messerschmitt, who had walked along the tunnel to see the production of his aircraft engines, replied, "No concentration camp inmates, as far as I know. But perhaps I wasn't paying much attention to the matter."

All perceptions are subjective: Josef Ackermann, who had been summoned to Nuremberg to give evidence in the secondary trial of the SS economists who controlled output in the concentration camps, had seen a very different state of affairs in Dora-Mittelbau.

There had indeed been a very high level of secrecy in the tunnel. However, as he was working in the sick bay, the journalist could move relatively freely. "When I was going along the galleries," he said during his interrogation in Nuremberg, "I had to keep climbing over bodies. They lay in the middle of the path." Many camp inmates had died of exhaustion as they worked. "The misery of the prisoners down there in the galleries was unimaginable." About fifty thousand camp inmates worked in Dora, most of them foreigners. Many of them slept in huge stone chambers inside the underground complex and never breathed fresh air for weeks on end. There was no water for washing, and the prisoners' skin was soon entirely encrusted with dust from the stone. "The prisoners," said Ackermann, "had to resort to pissing on their hands and using their urine to wash their faces."

The journalist also kept the records of deaths in Dora, so he could give an accurate assessment of the monthly death rate. In March 1945, the month when Messerschmitt visited the camp, five thousand people had died, according to Ackermann's reckoning, one tenth of all inmates. They usually died of exhaustion. Because the two incinerators in the camp were unable to cope with such a quantity of dead bodies, large fires were lit outside the galleries to burn the corpses. You could smell the stench of it miles away—something else that Willy Messerschmitt claimed not to have noticed.

This part of the story was presumably not mentioned at the Witness House. Here, that nice aircraft constructor was very popular. He was even forgiven for boring the other guests on occasion with his endless lectures on space flight. And the company present in the Witness House would not have encouraged Josef Ackermann to spoil the mood by giving his version of events. All the same, in the visitors' book Willy Messerschmitt bewailed "these hard times" when "envy, hatred, and resentment guide the fate of mankind, and kindness is so seldom found"—he praised the "attentive care" of the lady of the house all the more warmly for that.

Messerschmitt came back to the Witness House several times. Ackermann, however, stayed in Novalisstrasse for only three days. On April 24, 1947, he gave evidence in the fourth subsidiary trial held by the American military court, the trial of Oswald Pohl and other SS officers working for the SS Economics and Administrative Department.* All the physical exploitation of concentration camp inmates was organized by that department, and a number of industrial firms and manufacturing works, including Messerschmitt's, profited extensively from its operations.

Ackermann made no entry in the visitors' book. However, we learn from a small newspaper article published a little later that, sitting with Messerschmitt at the dining table in Novalisstrasse that evening, he "could hardly get the food in his mouth down."

Oblivion, distortion, whitewashing—that was the behavioral pattern whereby many tried to put the past behind them as quickly as possible in the immediate postwar period. The amnesia of fellow travelers and those who had colluded with the Nazis assumed such proportions that it became too much even for Diels, the former Gestapo man. He was particularly annoyed to find the former Nazi officials present in Nuremberg trying to make out that they had been whiter than white all along. Now that he was no longer under house arrest, he sometimes mingled with the guests in the living room of the villa, and he had heard the terms in which a few once-prominent

---

* There were eighteen defendants in this trial. Pohl and three others were sentenced to death, three more were acquitted, and the rest received prison sentences of varying length.

Party men spoke of him. "That man Diels has given us nothing but trouble," said one ministerial adviser. Diels promptly passed this remark on to his friends in the CIC.

As a result, American military police suddenly stormed the Witness House on February 3, 1947. They thundered up the stairs and took custody of a man who had come to Novalisstrasse in the character of a minor civil servant. This was Walter Letsch, once an adviser in the Ministry of Labor under Fritz Sauckel, who had been condemned to death in the trial of the leading war criminals. The adviser had organized and managed the recruitment of forced labor in the occupied eastern countries, where the methods of local "recruiting officers," as Letsch later frankly admitted under interrogation, had increasingly involved force of arms. Many of the local entrepreneurs had opposed these practices, and they had been supported by Diels in his capacity as director of the shipping department of the Hermann Göring Works from 1940, and who traveled widely at the time in the Balkans and other countries east of the Danube.

On his travels, Rudolf Diels had learned about the concentration camps at an early date. He had heard of systematic shootings, and he had seen the mass grave at Babi Yar near Kiev in Ukraine. "If you kept your eyes and ears open," he kept saying at the villa in Novalisstrasse, "you could get to know what game the Nazis were playing early on." He reacted all the more angrily to the attempts at exoneration so common now in the Witness House, where many of the guests persistently claimed to have known nothing at all.

Walter Letsch was presumably not the only one denounced by Diels and then arrested, although the deciding factor may well have been that the Americans had found his initials on the minutes of a meeting where the mass killing of Russian prisoners of war was discussed. Gritting his teeth, the civil servant remembered, under pressure and in view of the weight of evidence, that he had indeed been present at that meeting. He added zealously, however: "But I can't remember any figures or other details now."

CANDY AND ZYKLON B

Eugen Kogon was exhausted, downcast—and perhaps also embittered. The writer and journalist was driven back to the Witness House in a U.S. jeep late in the afternoon of April 23, 1947, after spending seven hours in the courtroom telling the dreadful tale of life and death in the Buchenwald concentration camp. It had been like a battle. Kogon repeatedly faced trick questions from the defense counsel. "I am being made to feel like a stupid boy!" he finally exclaimed angrily. However, the worst was yet to come. One of the lawyers defending a particularly brutal SS functionary even accused the journalist of complicity in many of the murders at Buchenwald himself because, as the prisoner who kept records in the sick bay of the concentration camp, he had been obliged to watch them.

It was a world turned upside down. During the Nazi period Eugen Kogon had spent seven years in captivity, and then, through a daring act, had made sure that the Americans could reach Buchenwald in April 1945, just in time to keep the Nazis from murdering the last prisoners. Now he was sitting at the same table as former Krupp managers, high-ranking employees of IG Farben, and Messerschmitt the aircraft constructor, a long-term and welcome guest in Novalisstrasse. Another gentleman, of rather strange appearance, had joined the company.

He was said to have been an adjutant to the much-feared head of the Nazi Chancellery, Martin Bormann.

The majority of these men had presumably had a hand in the murder of many thousands of human beings, or had at least profited by it, yet they were cheerfully living at liberty and enjoying the hospitality of the Witness House. It was not the first time that Eugen Kogon had been here. The Americans had put him up at the villa on the outskirts of town for a few days some months earlier, so he knew the household routine. After supper Annemarie von Kleist, the lady of the house, usually brought out cards for a game of bridge, or some of the gentlemen would sit over the popular game of skat. "Eighteen, twenty—I pass." How often the writer had already heard that in the Witness House. Kogon himself was not particularly fond of such card games.

And now he, an intellectual, had to put up with public accusations of double-dealing in the courtroom, blamed for standing by inactive when murder was committed. The Nuremberg lawyer Eduard Belzer had attacked him in the Palace of Justice that day, April 23, addressing him directly in a cutting voice. "Herr Kogon, as a witness you have told us that you knew about these murders." Why, the defense lawyer went on to ask the journalist with an accusatory tone, had he not gone immediately to the management of the camp to ask to be released from his position keeping records in the sick bay? Kogon was stunned. "Is a man to blame for knowing about murders in a concentration camp where they were being committed daily, from morning to evening, right, left, and center?" he shouted at the court, infuriated. Then he lowered his voice and added, "I suppose the correct course of conduct would have been for me to request my release from the concentration camp entirely."

At that an awkward silence fell on the courtroom. Every one of his hearers was well aware that such a contingency was utterly impossible for a concentration camp inmate. But the Nuremberg attorney had no grasp of irony. "So you do not consider yourself in any way complicit?" insisted Belzer. Now at last the presiding judge cut this remarkable interrogation short, declaring the question inadmissible, for after all, as he said, the witness was "not among the defendants."

Eugen Kogon's sufferings had begun on March 11, 1938, the night when the Gestapo had arrested him in Vienna. After studying sociology and political economy, Kogon had worked first as a writer, then as a property manager. From 1934 onward he had been general agent for the Prince of Saxe-Coburg-Gotha-Kohary, managing the financial profits of the prince's extensive possessions—mines, engineering works, other firms on his demesnes—which were mainly situated in Austria and Hungary, although some were in Germany and Czechoslovakia. A Catholic of liberal opinions, Kogon did a great deal of traveling, and in this way he made use of his position to inform like-minded people about what was going on in Germany, and to organize resistance to the National Socialist regime. However, the Nazis had learned of his activities, and so the prince's financial agent was already on the list to be arrested when Hitler annexed Austria in the Anschluss of March 1938.

Kogon stayed in the Gestapo prison in Vienna for over a year, and was then moved to Buchenwald in September 1939. There he was first assigned to a troop of men who did the hardest of labor in appalling and inhuman conditions. Kogon was soon suffering from suppurating abscesses all over his hands and feet. A thin, frail intellectual who had hardly any reserves of physical strength for such punishing work, and also wore glasses, he would have been unlikely to survive in the camp if he had not been transferred to the tailors' workshop in May 1941. Two years later, in June 1943, Kogon finally became a clerk working for the SS doctor Erwin Ding-Schuler, who had set up a laboratory for experiments with typhus. In his new post, Kogon gradually came to know the entire structure of the camp, and indeed of the SS administrative system as a whole.

Like many other concentration camp doctors in Dachau and Auschwitz, Dr. Ding-Schuler used his position at Buchenwald to carry out experiments on human beings, which usually ended in death. Prisoners were subjected to various kinds of pathogens designed to infect them with typhus or jaundice, smallpox or paratyphoid fever. The doctor experimented with hormones, various poisonous substances, and phosphorus bombs. Meanwhile, however, Kogon succeeded in winning Ding-Schuler's confidence, and as a result he himself gained more and more knowledge of top secret correspondence. In April 1945, when the U.S. army was coming closer and closer, and the SS in Buchenwald was already beginning to wipe out its traces and kill prisoners en masse, Kogon even persuaded the doctor to smuggle him out of the camp. Ding-Schuler had the prisoner nailed down in a crate of medicaments and taken to his own villa in nearby Weimar. There Kogon got out of the crate, using tools that he had brought with him, and made his way to the Americans, who had already reached Jena. Although the U.S. soldiers had other plans, he convinced them to move fast on Buchenwald, and they liberated the camp on April 11, 1945.

Buchenwald was the first large camp to fall into the hands of the U.S. troops almost intact. A few days after its liberation, therefore, an investigation team came to the Ettersberg area where the camp stood to study it. Kogon and a group of other prisoners were asked to draw up a report on conditions there. Now, two years later almost to the day, several leading members of the SS were on the defendants' bench in Nuremberg, and Kogon was being questioned about details of life in the camp. He described the triangular badges of different colors that prisoners had to wear on their clothing—red for political prisoners, green for criminals, yellow for Jews, pink for homosexuals. He talked about the daily roll calls, often lasting for hours, when the prisoners were ordered "Caps off!" or "Caps on!" again and again, and everyone feared being called "to the gate" because that could mean a death sentence.

A prisoner might be arbitrarily punished and even killed for no reason at all, or on absurd pretexts, for instance for having a button missing from his jacket, supposedly giving an SS man an insolent look, or failing to keep his hand straight enough against the seam of his pants. Then the prisoner had to climb on a "horse" to the left of the gate, where he was publicly whipped. Other offenders were taken to the bunker. "You could be starved to death there," Kogon told the court, "or you could be fed on salt herring but given no water until you went out of your mind, you could be hung up by your feet." The prisoners could never tell in advance what might happen. "You lived in constant fear of being the next victim," said Kogon.

Finally, there was a special device for shooting people in the back of the neck at Buchenwald. It was in what were called "the stables," and appeared to be a harmless measuring device. The prisoner had to stand on a platform that looked, at first glance, as if it were meant to measure his height. In fact, however, he would be shot in the back of the neck through a hole in the measuring chart on the board behind him, while loud voices were broadcast through loudspeakers placed all around the device to drown out the sound of the shot. "Nine thousand to nine and a half thousand Russian prisoners," Kogon estimated in the courtroom, had been killed in Buchenwald alone. Many of them had arrived expecting to be better off here than in a POW camp.

Even when he was in the tailors' workshop of the concentration camp, the writer had realized that people must have been dying en masse since 1942 outside the camp as well, in numbers of a magnitude far exceeding those in Buchenwald. More and more consignments of clothing kept arriving at the tailors' workshop from Auschwitz and other places in the east. Some of the garments were bloodstained; others had holes in them from gunshots. Many of the clothes bore a yellow Jewish star, but it was even more alarming that the shirts and jackets came with marks inside them from tailors' shops all over Europe—something on a large scale was definitely afoot. While he was working for Dr. Ding-Schuler, a set of statistics relating to deaths fell into Kogon's hands. According to those statistics, from June to November 1942, within a period of six months, eighty thousand prisoners had died in camps like Buchenwald alone. At that time Kogon could not have known any details of figures from the death camps themselves.

Buchenwald, like other camps of the same type, was supposed to make a profit. Consequently, the death rate in these camps was too high even for the SS men in charge. Orders were issued from Berlin to the camp doctors to ensure that "the labor force of the prisoners is used to better effect for manufacturing armaments," as Kogon told the tribunal in Nuremberg. He had salvaged the camp doctor's secret duty journal from Buchenwald, and it now played an important part in the trial of the SS leaders, as it already had in the Doctors' Trial a few months earlier. The book contained much material to incriminate the defendants in both trials—and for that very reason the defense lawyers did all they could to cast doubt on the credibility of Kogon's evidence and present Dr. Ding-Schuler's journal as a forgery.

Kogon, now forty-four years old, was already famous in Germany at the time. His account of Buchenwald had been published in book form in December 1946 under the title of *Der SS-Staat* (The SS State), and was soon translated into several languages, appearing in English as *The Theory and Practice of Hell*. It became one of the most read books of the postwar period. In 1946 Kogon had also founded the *Frankfurter Hefte*, a critical monthly journal that soon became, as it were, the intellectual conscience of Germany. Kogon had been living with his family in Oberursel, near Frankfurt, since the summer of 1945, close to one of the American interrogation centers, and he got on extremely well with the occupying forces.

However, when the writer first came to Nuremberg in January 1947, he was rather shocked. A U.S. jeep had fetched him from Oberursel. There was already an engineer in the vehicle who had also been summoned for questioning in Nuremberg. This man had a great deal to tell, as Kogon found out during the drive and later at the Witness House, where he and the engineer were both staying. "It turned out that he had piped Zyklon B into the gas chambers."

Directly after the war Kogon had described the system of the concentration camps in minute detail. However, the overall plan for carrying out the mass killings in the death camps like Auschwitz, Treblinka, and Sobibor was not yet known. The Nazis usually kept the most meticulous records of everything, and so some of the U.S. prosecutors in Nuremberg assumed that there must also have been a Nazi scenario for the tragedy of the gas chambers somewhere in the files. Around the turn of the year 1946 to 1947, Robert Kempner had been given the job of preparing for a secondary trial of particularly prominent Nazi ministerial officials. He was now looking for incriminating material to clarify the responsibility of those officials. Kempner set his team to work in Berlin. A relatively large number of letters sent to the Foreign Office by SS offices such as the

Reich Central Security Office had already fallen into American hands, and Kempner had a feeling that there must still be some relevant documents to be found in the diplomatic offices.

One of Kempner's bloodhounds was Eddi I. Wahler, a Jew born in Frankfurt who had emigrated from Germany in 1934 at the age of sixteen. Wahler spent four months in Berlin in 1947 to collect material evidence for the later Wilhelmstrasse Trial*—"I followed all kinds of trails," said Wahler, "but everything was in total confusion." I met him, now an old gentleman, at his apartment in central Hesse. A man with large brown eyes and a nearly bald head opened the door for me. He was eighty-seven years old, had been living in Germany for several years when I visited him, and had a small private archive in his home, kept in his bedroom closet, containing several copies of documents that he had found at the time. Most of them were ancient, very thick photocopies that made a dull sound if you tried folding them. The pages of text were black like a negative—that was how photocopies looked then.

"At the time we searched various offices," the old gentleman said. The U.S. troops had taken some of the documentary material they seized to a former Gestapo villa beside the Krumme Lanke lake in the south of Berlin, "built partly underground." The Foreign Office papers went elsewhere, to be stored in various places, "the files up to 1943 in the West, the later ones in the East." Robert Kempner's search team finally found what they were looking for in the building of the Telefunken Company in Berlin-Lichterfelde. A pink file inscribed on the front "Final Solution for the Jewish Problem" fell into their hands in

---

* So called because the German Foreign Office was in Wilhelmstrasse, Berlin, but also known as the Ministries Trial. This was the eleventh of the secondary Nuremberg trials.

March 1947. "Unfortunately I didn't discover the file myself," said Wahler. "An Englishwoman came upon it."

The file was immediately flown to Nuremberg, where Kempner received the documents with satisfaction. They were the minutes of the Wannsee Conference, as we now call it, to which the head of the SS Security Service, Reinhard Heydrich, had invited the state secretaries of the various National Socialist ministries on January 23, 1942. More than a dozen top officials of the Third Reich were present that icy January morning, at a grand villa belonging to the Security Service, number 56–58 Am Grossen Wannsee, along a lake just outside the gates of Berlin, when Heydrich set out the details of his systematic plan for disposing of the Jews. The first transports had driven east long before, and there were already several death camps available, but they had not been able to make up their minds about the manner of the intended slaughter of the Jews. At Chelmo, near Lodz, three gas vans for killing by means of carbon monoxide poisoning had been in use since December 1941, and in Auschwitz, in the fall of that same year, the first experiments with Zyklon B had been made, while in Belzec, near Lublin, the gas chambers were only just being constructed.

As early as July 1941, Heydrich had been instructed by Reich Marshal Göring to work out a plan for the liquidation of the Jews. In the archive that he kept, Wahler described finding material relevant to this order. Since September 1941, all Jewish inhabitants in the countries under German rule had been forced to wear a yellow star sewn to their jackets. At Wannsee, Heydrich now wanted the assembled civil service heads of the Nazi Reich to give their blessing to his appalling plan and make the leaders of National Socialist bureaucracy his accomplices in murder.

The meeting clearly went entirely to Heydrich's satisfaction. As it drew to a close, cognac and open sandwiches were served, while the gentlemen casually discussed the advantages and disadvantages of various methods of killing. After that Heydrich's right-hand man, Adolf Eichmann, drew up the five-page minutes of the meeting, and presumably copies of it were sent a few weeks later to all participants. As stated in the minutes, a total of eleven million Jews were to be killed. Precise figures were given of how many were expected to die from which countries.

As the cover page of the minutes that arrived at the Foreign Office on February 26, 1942, shows, there were thirty copies of this document, each of them numbered. The copy discovered among the papers in the Foreign Office bore the number 16. It was to be the only copy of this murderous record ever discovered; no trace was ever found of the other copies. Aware of the explosive nature of that meeting, obviously all the other participants in the plan had destroyed their copies of the minutes in good time before the Allied forces marched in, but the representative from the Foreign Office had been unable to do the same because, shortly before the end of the war, he had been removed from his post for various misdemeanors. On the cover of the copy that was found, the names of all who attended the meeting were listed.

Kempner was particularly interested in the role of the Foreign Office in the Nazi regime. Its representative at the Wannsee Conference, however, Undersecretary Martin Luther, head of the department for Germany, had now died in Russian captivity in 1945. So the U.S. prosecutor remembered an official who had already given evidence at the main trial, and had been in the witnesses' wing of the courthouse prison for some time. This was the Foreign Office lawyer Friedrich Gaus. Now sixty-six years old, he had drawn up treaties for the pre-Nazi foreign minister Stresemann, and later he was also responsible for the phrasing of the Hitler-Stalin pact. This treaty, which contravened international law, had already come under discussion at the main trial, and Kempner made use of that fact to bring pressure to bear on the diplomat. The prosecutor made it clear to the German administrator that he could be handed over to the Russians himself—and there was nothing that Gaus feared more.

The diplomat therefore proved surprisingly cooperative. As a token of goodwill, Gaus was given a bed at the Witness House in Novalisstrasse, and from then on was allowed to consider himself a "voluntary witness." Kempner also had another top diplomat brought to Nuremberg: Ernst von Weizsäcker, former state secretary in the Foreign Office. He too had given evidence at the main trial and had to be summoned directly from Rome, where he had been ambassador to the Holy See and continued to enjoy the Vatican's hospitality after the end of the war. At that time Weizsäcker had been giving evidence for the defense, but now his interrogation was to be considerably more unpleasant.

The former state secretary arrived at the Witness House in March 1947. He does not seem to have been particularly pleased to find his old Foreign Office colleague Friedrich Gaus there. In the courthouse, where Kempner kept pitting the two diplomats against each other, they were constantly disagreeing—and presumably the U.S. prosecutor, who himself had trained at the Prussian Interior Ministry, followed the course of their quarrels with some satisfaction. In the Witness House, the two top diplomats tried to avoid each other. They had been acquainted for more than twenty years and had once, as Weizsäcker said, been relatively close, but now they were in the business of blackening each other's character to Kempner.

Weizsäcker said, for instance, that Gaus had been in favor of war against Britain from the start, adding that the lawyer had acted as "Ribbentrop's inquisitor" at the Foreign Office: "He was always in pursuit" of those whom the foreign minister could blame when things went wrong, said Weizsäcker in one session under questioning by Kempner, which was probably the reason for the other man's reputation as the "evil genius" of the Foreign Office, as some described him. In another interrogation, Gaus struck back when the subject turned to Weizsäcker's membership in the SS. Of necessity, the former state secretary had to admit to having worn the uniform "from time to time—although only on certain days," for instance at the Nuremberg Party rallies. Gaus, on the other hand, said that sometimes the baron had even worn the black SS uniform at the office for no perceptible reason. "I was horrified," added the lawyer.

Kempner summoned Weizsäcker to the courtroom daily at the end of March 1947, and the rope was slowly tightening around the neck of the former National Socialist diplomat. Of course the prosecutor also had the evidence of the one-time state secretary checked after his interrogations, for Weizsäcker, as Kempner later recollected in his memoirs, had not always been entirely honest with him. On the way to the Witness House the diplomat had once remarked to the soldier escorting him that he thought he had lied very well to the gentleman interrogating him that day.

Other men who had their own ideas of what the truth meant, honest as they might claim to be, stayed at the Witness House at this rime. There was Edinger Ancker, for instance, a former colleague of Martin Bormann, head of the Nazi Chancellery, who had exerted increasing influence on Hitler in the last years of the Third Reich. Ancker arrived at the Witness House on March 28, 1947. He was a North German lawyer, aged thirty-six, who had been responsible in Bormann's Chancellery for the delicate matter of "racial questions." Now, by his own account, he was earning his living as a farmhand.

A former SS Obersturmbannführer, he was soon being interrogated daily at the Palace of Justice in Nuremberg, but there seemed to be a great many gaps in his memory. Ancker could no longer recollect having explicitly backed a tightening up of the laws on the confiscation of Jewish property. He had also clearly had a hand in passing other laws designed to legitimize the increasingly harsh persecution of those of his fellow citizens who happened to be Jews. However, in conversation with the U.S. official interrogating him, Ancker merely shrugged his shoulders: "I really can't explain that now."

He also claimed to know nothing about the conference on the "Final Solution of the Jewish Problem." However, what Heydrich had first said at the state secretaries' level was reiterated by Adolf Eichmann a little later to the departmental heads of the Nazi bureaucracy. On March 6, 1942, he met them at Kurfürstenstrasse, Berlin, and Edinger Ancker was one of those present. The meeting covered technical and administrative problems in carrying out the most wide-reaching plan to commit murder ever designed in the course of history. One subject of debate was the treatment of so-called "mongrels," meaning the offspring of mixed Jewish and non-Jewish parents and grandparents. In Nuremberg Ancker at first claimed to remember nothing about this meeting, but the Americans finally managed to extract from him an admission that he had indeed been present. Asked for details of the discussion, however, Ancker claimed: "I'd be lying if I said I knew anything about it."

In the eyes of the Americans, SS Obersturmbannführer Edinger Ancker, who stayed at the Witness House from March to May 1947, was only a little fish, so they did not press him further. Matters were rather different with Weizsäcker, a prominent figure. In addition, a document had now surfaced that deeply incriminated the former state secretary in the Foreign Office. Weizsäcker had not only initialed a note arranging for the deportation of six thousand French Jews to Auschwitz, he had also corrected the content of the text by adding a handwritten remark to the effect that those liable for deportation should be "the Jews to whom police attention has most closely been drawn." In addition, he changed the phrasing of a comment that there would be "no reservations" on the part of the Foreign Office to say that the Foreign Office would "raise no objection."

"Do you know Auschwitz?" Kempner asked the diplomat at Nuremberg in the spring of 1947. Weizsäcker replied: "To be honest with you, I don't even know where it is."

Weizsäcker used to mark official documents with a finely traced "W" in brown pencil; the initial that he had inscribed on the note about the French Jews on March 20, 1942 was later to be his undoing. But his initials also appeared on other documents to do with the murder of Jews, and recent investigations into his involvement in the deportation of ninety thousand European Jews to Auschwitz are considered to prove his guilt, as Ulrich Völklein writes in his book *Die Weizsäckers* (The Weizsäckers). Weizsäcker's mark is even said to have been found on a cover letter to the Wannsee minutes that arrived at the Foreign Office at the end of February 1942, although the paper cannot be located today.

Robert Kempner had the diplomat driven home again in the spring of 1947. A few weeks later Ernst von Weizsäcker was arrested, and later at the Wilhelmstrasse Trial he was sentenced to seven years' imprisonment. However, his entry of April 2, 1947, in the visitors' book of the Witness House sounds both appreciative and confident: "It was like being in Heaven here."

After a gap of many years, I went back to the Hotel Sonnenhof in Königstein in the summer of 2005. The armchairs in
the beautiful old villa were as worn as they had been when I
had met Kempner there in 1987. I was going to meet Cornelia
Ebeling, Eugen Kogon's daughter. At my request, she had spent
weeks going through her father's literary estate, and she did
indeed find an account of the Witness House that he had written. It showed that in 1947 Kogon complained to the Americans about conditions at the villa. The document consisted of
a few very thin sheets of paper, already fraying slightly, the
kind used in those days for carbon copies. The type was blue.
Kogon criticized the sparse diet provided for the "eight to sixteen persons" staying at the Witness House at the beginning of
1947. Breakfast, he said, had consisted of a thin slice of white
bread, and on alternate days a small portion of porridge, or a
pancake, or a fried egg. There were none of those fortifying
little items that made life to some extent worth living, he said,
such as tobacco products or candy.

Kogon did not write in detail about the guests, but only mentioned the harsh American practice of fetching them, which he
himself had experienced. Before being driven into Nuremberg,
the witnesses were often told briefly and brusquely that they
were needed, no more than that, so that most of them had no
idea what it was about. In Nuremberg they were then often
"much surprised" because "their questioning usually lasted for
a long time"—and as a rule surprise gave way to increasing
annoyance. Only once did Kogon indicate how uncomfortable
he obviously really did find conditions at the Witness House.
"Since former political prisoners are well acquainted with the
practices of the Gestapo in its time," as Kogon cautiously expressed it in his well-phrased text, "relevant comparisons are
made and expressed." But "this whole affair," said the writer

the next moment, playing his criticism down again, was in itself ridiculous by comparison with what "is at stake for the witnesses in the main business." It must therefore, he thought, be easy to put these matters right. Kogon's main attention was bent on the light that the trials would cast on the recent past, and he concentrated on that with all his might.

Directly after the war, his daughter Cornelia Ebeling told me at the Hotel Sonnenhof as we looked out the window at the panorama of the valley below, her father had come to terms well with his terrible experiences in the concentration camp. "I made sociology out of them," the writer himself said once. Years later, however, his daughter told me, he had been tormented by nightmares. "He would rage and hit out in the night," and her mother had found it hard to bear these nocturnal fits.

Even in 1980, as Kogon once said in a television interview, he still suffered from such nightmares. He described powerfully to the camera how much the suffering he had undergone in the past still tormented him. This was at about the time when my own father finally broke his silence and told me about his experiences during the period when the National Socialists held power. That was the evening when our long-term guest Bernhard also brought out the old visitors' book from the Witness House, the book that first aroused my curiosity.

AFTERWORD

Many stories never come to an end, and much more could be said about the Witness House. It remained open until the fall of 1948, and in the last months of its existence the entries in the visitors' book show that the Kleists had moved to another villa, also in the Erlenstegen district of Nuremberg, which they went on managing as a guesthouse. One of the last signatures in the visitors' book is that of Hitler's former adjutant Fritz Wiedemann. "I leave . . . with renewed faith in the future of Germany," he wrote on September 7, 1948.

By this time Countess Kálnoky had already left Germany. She had gone first to Austria, and then, in 1949, emigrated with her family to the United States. On their arrival in Boston the family was photographed by a newspaper reporter, and the picture was later captioned, in large letters: IN FLIGHT FROM COMMUNISM. Their crossing to the States had been arranged by a Catholic aid organization, the War Relief Services of the National Catholic Welfare Conference. Its European director, based in Vienna, was the countess's old acquaintance Fabian Flynn, and it is possible that he helped with their move. The priest himself was soon to go to Hungary, where he organized American aid for several years.

Meanwhile Ingeborg Kálnoky and her husband were trying to make a life in the New World under difficult conditions. On their arrival each member of the family was given two dollars.

First the Kálnokys worked on a chicken farm, then they went
to Washington, D.C., where the countess found a job as a
housemaid while her husband was a cleaner in an art gallery.
Later the count entered the service of the Library of Congress
as a translator, and he died of kidney cancer in 1955. Ingeborg
Kálnoky lived in Alabama for a long time; her children's former nursemaid Cuci was part of the household. The countess
spent the last years of her life in that small apartment in Cleveland, Ohio, near her daughter Lori's home. She died in 1997.

Very few of the guests at the Witness House are still alive
today. The first of them to die was Karl Haushofer, who committed suicide in 1946. Hitler's photographer Heinrich Hoffmann died in 1957. Before that, he had been classified as a
major offender in a denazification court, and was condemned
to ten years in a labor camp and forbidden to practice his profession for the same length of time. He was also' ordered to
surrender his fortune, which had been assessed at about nine
million Reichsmarks. He appealed this sentence, and in 1953
had it quashed, along with the ban on practicing his profession. Ultimately he was also left in possession of his fortune,
although in the turmoil of the end of the war its value seems to
have reduced considerably from the original estimate.

Rudolf Diels died in a hunting accident in 1957. He had
left his gun on the backseat of his car with the safety catch off;
his dog jumped on it, it went off, and the incorrigible woman-
izer Diels, former head of the Gestapo, was hit in the stomach.
There was all manner of speculation about his death, for Diels
had kept himself in the public eye by publishing many books
and articles in which he put forward provocative theories, for
instance about the Reichstag fire (an event that he had wit-
nessed firsthand), or matters to do with the secret service.

In 1993 Robert Kempner died in his usual room at the Hotel Sonnenhof, where he had stayed to the last. His assistant, Jane Lester, stayed on for a few years in her apartment in Oberursel, where she managed a large part of Kempner's literary estate. I often visited her there, and looked through those of Kempner's papers that were later to go into the archives. Kempner, who was in charge of the prosecution at the Wilhelmstrasse Trial, stayed in Nuremberg until the end of the 1940s. His colleague Drexel Sprecher, who acted as chief prosecutor in the IG Farben Trial, also went on working in Franconia for several years longer. "I was one of the first to arrive and one of the last to leave," he told me in Washington.

After his spectacular appearance at the trial of the major war criminals in November 1945, Erwin Lahousen was almost forgotten as a prisoner of war. When he was moved from the Witness House, he was transferred to new accommodations several times. Lahousen appeared once more as a witness in Nuremberg, at the secondary trial of several Wehrmacht generals thought to have been very deeply involved in the machinations of the Nazis. In June 1947 he was released from POW status and went to the Tyrol, where after the death of his first wife he married again in 1953. Two years later, in February 1955, Lahousen died of a heart attack.

The aircraft constructor Willy Messerschmitt had to undergo interrogation in Nuremberg several times up to July 1947, but never actually appeared as a witness in any of the trials. Classified a "fellow traveler" by a denazification court, he soon went back to designing aircraft, this time for the Federal German Armed Forces. After several mergers, the aircraft company he had founded became Messerschmitt-Bölkow-Blohm PLC. Messerschmitt died in 1978.

The lawyer Otto Kranzbühler was one of the last of the more prominent guests at the Witness House to die, in 2004, at the age of ninety-seven. After his successful defense of the last Reich president, Grand Admiral Karl Dönitz, Kranzbühler was one of the most sought-after lawyers in the related trials. He appeared for the defense in the Flick Trial. At the trial of managers of the Krupp company, he defended the head of the firm, Alfred Krupp von Bohlen und Halbach.

Several of the guests at the Witness House had spent such a short time in Novalisstrasse that their memories of the place seemed to consist merely of brief images when I talked to them—like a flashlight illuminating a scene for a fleeting instant. However, Gerhard Krülle, son of the owner of the house in Novalisstrasse, showed that his memory was excellent. Of course, as he was only a teenager at the time, he had been far younger than any of the guests. The U.S. soldier Richard Sonnenfeldt had also been one of the few really young people to have anything to do with the Witness House, and his memories gave me important information about individual witnesses and the house as a whole. Another of the young people at the time was Kempner's researcher Eddi Wahler. I would like to thank Krülle and Wahler, and, posthumously, Richard Sonnenfeldt (who died in 2009), for their willingness to tell me about their memories, and all the other witnesses of that time, both living and dead, whom I consulted, for their valuable information and the interesting discussions that I had with them.

I am particularly grateful to the children of Ingeborg Countess Kálnoky, for their trust in me, the useful tips and personal information that they gave me, and also for the pleasant time that I spent with them. For that, and for much else, I would like to express my sincere thanks to Lori Bongiovanni, Fárkas Count Kálnoky, and Ingeborg Despres-Kálnoky. I would

also like to thank Michael Kogon and Cornelia Ebeling, Eugen
Kogon's children, for going to the trouble of looking through
their father's literary estate on my behalf for mentions of the
Witness House. My thanks too to Count Anton-Wolfgang von
Faber-Castell for his willingness to give me useful information,
and to Thomas Ginsburger, son of the French Auschwitz survivor Marie-Claude Vaillant-Couturier, for his valuable help.

For many years the Witness House in Erlenstegen remained
substantially unchanged, thanks to Elisabeth Kühnle. The niece
of the former owner Elise Krülle, she and her husband bought
the building in the 1950s and lived in it for a long time. I spent
many hours at the little villa on the outskirts of the wood with
her, and got to know almost every nook and cranny in the
place. Elisabeth Kühnle was fascinated by the eventful past of
her little house. At over ninety, she moved to a retirement home
in 2004, and I thank her for the many interesting stories she
was able to tell me about the house. After she moved out it was
partially renovated, and a Nuremberg family now lives in it.

When one is reconstructing the past, the work consists of
taking many small steps, fitting piece after piece together as
if making a mosaic. To give an overall picture of the situation at the Witness House, I have been able to fall back on a
great range of information: conversations with contemporary
witnesses, public archives and private papers, eyewitness reports, the correspondence of Countess Kálnoky, and of course
the visitors' books with which all my research began. Records
of what was said by witnesses under interrogation were a particularly useful additional source of information for me, and
not only in finding out why those concerned were in Nuremberg at the time, but also in giving me an idea of what they
were like and enabling me at least to begin guessing what they
may have felt at the time, both in the courthouse building and

at the Witness House. In my research for old documentary evidence and the records of interrogations, Gunther Friedrich at the Nuremberg State Archive was very helpful to me, and Axel Frohn searched the National Archives in Washington on my behalf for any records of possible bugging in the Witness House (in fact there seems to have been none), and looked at many other documents. I would like to thank them both for the work they did for me. A special thank-you also to Father Robert E. Carbonneau and, posthumously, to Father Fabiano Giorgini, the priests in charge of the archives of the Passionist order in Rome and the United States respectively.

Writing decades after the events described here, of course I have been unable to research every detail, and there are inevitable gaps. In addition errors may have crept in, some of the contemporary witnesses may have misrepresented matters in retrospect, and I know that I am not immune to making mistakes and drawing the wrong conclusions. If there are any such instances, I ask for the reader's forbearance. My wish was to discover the historical facts as best I could, arrange them in narrative order, and present them so that even people not closely acquainted with the history could understand them. Here I would like to express particularly warm thanks to Klaus Brill, who read the manuscript and made many valuable suggestions for improvements. I would also like to thank my publishers at Goldmann Verlag for their patience.

To the end I was motivated by the question of why, all things considered, life at the Witness House ran so smoothly. Why, in what was probably the most bizarre community of people to be gathered together in the immediate postwar period, was there no open hostility between the very different guests staying there? It may have been due in part to the social skills of Countess Kálnoky and her successor, Annemarie von Kleist.

However, it seems to me more likely that it expresses a phenomenon marking the entire postwar period: the absolute silence that came down like a somber veil over recent events, and for a very long time prevented any real confrontation with the past. Whether the guests in the house were former Nazis, their fellow travelers, or their surviving victims, none of them could or would speak really frankly about their experiences. Guilt weighed down too heavily on some. Others lived with memories so terrible that there were no words to express them.

The concentration camp system, wrote Eugen Kogon in the first edition of his book in 1946, had been a jungle returning to the wild—and the perpetrators of Nazi atrocities and their victims alike were lost in that jungle. It is to their credit that the Americans, through their intensive research just after the war, turned the floodlights on the worst crimes of the Nazi regime. However, no one could absolve the Germans from the necessity of confronting their own past; they had to learn how to come to terms with it for themselves. We know that it was decades before a majority of the German people not only understood that but took it to heart. Only then was the time right to lift the opaque veil of silence from the past.

THE STAFF OF THE WITNESS HOUSE, U.S. MILITARY PERSONNEL, AND LONG-TERM INHABITANTS OF THE HOUSE

INGEBORG COUNTESS KÁLNOKY

First manager of the Witness House. Born Ingeborg von Breitenbuch in Metz, 1909, grew up at Ranis Castle in Thuringia, married Hugo Count Kálnoky in 1934, and then lived in Transylvania in Romania, later in Budapest. Escaped to Nuremberg in 1945 and was recruited by the Americans to run the Witness House. Kálnoky gave notice in Nuremberg in January 1947, and in 1949 went to the United States, where she died in 1997.

HUGO COUNT KÁLNOKY

Husband of Ingeborg Kálnoky. Born 1900 in Vienna, lived first in Transylvania, then in Budapest, where he worked as an editor and translator. Was reunited with his wife in Nuremberg in 1947, and in 1949 went with her and their four children—Eleonora, Fárkas, Antony, and Ingeborg—to the United States, where he died in 1955.

RUDOLF DIELS

First head of the Gestapo. Born 1900 at Berghausen in the Taunus, studied law in Marburg, became a senior civil servant in the Prussian Interior Ministry in 1930 under the Social Democrat Carl Severing. In 1933 Severing's successor Hermann Göring gave Diels the job of heading his newly founded Geheime Staatspolizei (Secret State Police), the Gestapo. However, Diels had to resign his post in May 1934 after a power struggle between Göring and Heinrich Himmler. He became administrative head of the Cologne governmental district, moved to the same position in Hanover in 1935, and was later head of the shipping department of the Hermann Göring Works. He was taken into custody during the wave of arrests following the July Plot against Hitler's life in 1944, and stayed there until January 1945. Diels died in a hunting accident in 1957.

HEINRICH HOFFMANN

Hitler's personal photographer. Born 1885 in Fürth, Bavaria. Opened a photographic studio in the Schwabing district of Munich in 1909. Joined the National Socialist Workers' Party (the Nazi Party) in 1920, took his first portrait photographs of Hitler in 1923. When the Nazis came to power in 1933 Hoffmann had what amounted to a monopoly on Hitler portraits. He called himself Reich photo-reporter, published many volumes of pictures of Hitler, started an illustrated magazine, and built up his photographic business into a flourishing publicity firm. Hoffmann died in Munich in 1957.

ROBERT M. W. KEMPNER

Deputy to chief prosecutor Robert Jackson in the trial of the main war criminals, later chief prosecutor in the Wilhelmstrasse Trial. Born 1899 in Freiburg im Breisgau, grew up in Berlin, studied law in Freiburg. Worked first as a public prosecutor, moved in 1928 to the Prussian Interior Ministry, where he became lawyer to the police department. After the Nazis came to power in 1933, Kempner lost his job and was arrested in 1935. Set free again, he emigrated to the United States in 1939. After the war Kempner opened a legal office in Frankfurt, and appeared in many trials demanding rehabilitation and compensation for victims of the Nazis. He died at Königstein in 1993.

FABIAN FLYNN

U.S. army priest in Nuremberg. Born 1905 in Boston, joined the Passionist order, and in 1932 was ordained priest. Flynn worked first as an editor of the Catholic monthly magazine *The Sign*. From 1942 to 1946 was a military chaplain with the U.S. army. He received many decorations, and rose to the rank of major. After leaving the army he worked in aid organizations for refugees and was director of the National Catholic Relief Services in various parts of Europe. Back in the States, Flynn was public relations director of the Catholic Relief Services, New York, from 1961 to 1968. He died in 1973.

RICHARD SONNENFELDT

Interpreter for the U.S. prosecution team in Nuremberg. Born 1923 in Berlin, grew up in Gardelegen, near Magdeburg. Sonnenfeldt went to England at the age of fifteen and finally, during the war, made his way by an adventurous route to the United States. As a soldier in the U.S. army, Sonnenfeldt returned to Germany and was engaged by the prosecution in Nuremberg as an interpreter because of his fluent German. Sonnenfeldt made a career as a manager in the American media after the war, and lived on Long Island. He died in 2009.

Drexel Sprecher

A member of Robert Jackson's prosecution team, and chief prosecutor in the IG Farben Trial. Born 1913, studied law in Cambridge, Massachusetts. Sprecher, a distant cousin of Nina von Faber-Castell, was one of the prosecutors of Baldur von Schirach in the main Nuremberg trial. After the war, Sprecher lectured at Georgetown University, Washington, among other things. He died in 2006.

Elise Krülle

Owner of the house at number 24 Novalisstrasse. She worked as a housemaid in the Witness House. Born 1894 in Regensburg, trained as an inspector of taxes. Elise Krülle died in Nuremberg in 1952.

Gerhard Krülle

Son of Elise Krülle. He was thirteen when the Witness House was opened. Born in Nuremberg in 1932, studied mechanical engineering, and became professor of the technology of space flight. Krülle is now retired and lives near Stuttgart.

ANNEMARIE VON KLEIST

Second manager of the Witness House. Born 1907 in Dorpat, Estonia. In 1935 married Bernhard von Kleist, with whom she had two children. She died in Bonn in 1967.

BERNHARD VON KLEIST

U.S. interpreter at the time of the secondary Nuremberg trials, husband of Annemarie von Kleist. Born 1901 in Gross-Kössin, Pomerania, he worked as a businessman in the 1920s in Morocco, Venezuela, and Colombia. Returned to Europe in 1933, switched to farming, and took a lease on a farm near Riga. Fought at the front in the war. From 1946 acted as an interpreter in the various secondary trials in Nuremberg. After the war Kleist worked as an interpreter in the Ministry of Defense. He died in 1983 in Frankenberg an der Eder.

OTHER GUESTS AND VISITORS
AT THE WITNESS HOUSE

JOSEF ACKERMANN

Journalist and concentration camp prisoner held in Dachau, Buchenwald, and Dora-Mittelbau. Born 1896 in Munich, Ackermann worked as a journalist on various newspapers. Between 1933 and 1945 he was in prison almost continually, with short breaks, finally in the subterranean camp of Dora-Mittelbau, near Nordhausen, where the "retaliatory" V-2 rocket and various aircraft parts were assembled. Ackermann was head of the city press service in Munich after the war, and founded the *Münchner Stadtanzeiger* newspaper in 1948. He died in 1959.

EDINGER ANCKER

SS Obersturmbannführer and colleague of Martin Bormann. Born 1909 in Kiel, studied law in Hamburg, Vienna, and Berlin. Legal adviser in Kiel in 1933, and governmental assessor in the Altenkirchen district, Westerwald, in 1937. Worked with Martin Bormann in the Nazi Party Chancellery starting in 1942.

COUNTESS NINA VON FABER-CASTELL

Hostess of Dürrenhembach and friend of Rudolf Diels in their youth. Born 1916 in Küsnacht, Switzerland, as Katharina Sprecher von Bernegg, studied music in Berlin. In 1938 married Count Roland von Faber-Castell. She died in Switzerland in 1993.

HANS BERND GISEVIUS

Colleague of Rudolf Diels in the Prussian Interior Ministry. Later worked for the Abwehr. Born 1904 in Arnsberg, studied law in Berlin, Marburg, and Munich. Gisevius joined the National Socialist Party in February 1933, worked as departmental head at the Gestapo office in Berlin, and later went as vice-consul to Zürich, where he worked for the Abwehr department under Wilhelm Canaris, and at the same time made contacts with the American Office of Strategic Services (OSS). Gisevius died in Müllheim in Baden in 1974.

KARL HAUSHOFER

Geopolitician who inspired Hitler's policy of Lebensraum. Born 1869 in Munich, he pursued a military career to the rank of major general, was later a university professor of geopolitics, teacher of Rudolf Hess, and president of the popular League for the German Nation Abroad. Haushofer was in a concentration camp between July and August 1944 because of his son's involvement in the July Plot against Hitler. He committed suicide in 1946.

ROBERT HAVEMANN

Chemist and member of the Resistance to Hitler. Born 1910 in Munich, he studied chemistry. Havemann entered the Communist Party in 1932, and in 1942, with others, founded the "European Union" resistance group. In 1943 Havemann was arrested and condemned to death for high treason. While the execution of his sentence was postponed again and again, he was in prison in Brandenburg. After the war Havemann lived in the German Democratic Republic, and was later one of the best-known dissidents in its regime. He died in 1982.

EUGEN KOGON

Former prisoner in Buchenwald, writer and journalist. Born 1903 in Munich, Kogon studied political economy in Munich and Florence and completed his degree in Vienna. From 1924 Kogon was agent to the Prince of Saxe-Coburg-Gotha-Kohary. In 1938 he was sent to the Gestapo prison in Vienna, and was deported to Buchenwald a year later. He worked in the internal camp Resistance there. After the liberation of the camp, in the spring of 1945, the Americans asked him to write a report on it. The text became the basis of Kogon's book *Der SS-Staat*. After the war Kogon founded the *Frankfurter Hefte*. He was also one of the cofounders of the Christian Democratic Party, although he later turned against Konrad Adenauer's policy of restoration. Kogon died at Königstein in 1987.

OTTO KRANZBÜHLER

Defense lawyer in the main trial of the major war criminals. Born 1907, Kranzbühler studied law and was a naval judge during the war. In the main trial in Nuremberg he defended Grand Admiral Karl Dönitz. Later he appeared for Alfred Krupp von Bohlen und Halbach in the Krupp Trial. After the war Kranzbühler was a successful industrial lawyer. He died in the summer of 2004.

ERWIN LAHOUSEN VON VIVREMONT

Former Abwehr officer and the first prosecution witness of the main war criminals' trial in Nuremberg. Born 1896 in Vienna, he followed the career path of an army officer, and worked in the counterespionage department of the Austrian War Ministry. After the Austrian Anschluss, Lahousen joined the Abwehr under Admiral Wilhelm Canaris, and joined the Resistance to Hitler. Lahousen died in 1955.

GISELA LIMBERGER

Hermann Göring's librarian and private secretary. Born 1893, Limberger worked first as a secretary, then as a librarian in the Berlin State Library. In 1935 she moved to the staff office of then Prussian minister president Hermann Göring. She first organized and administered Göring's library, then cataloged his works of art, and after 1942 was his private secretary, dealing with all his private financial business.

WILLY EMIL MESSERSCHMITT

Aircraft constructor. Born 1898 in Frankfurt, Messerschmitt founded the Messerschmitt aircraft construction company, and built his first airplane, the Me 17, in 1923. In 1934 Messerschmitt designed the Me 109, the plane used more than any other in the Second World War by the German Luftwaffe. The aircraft constructor, appointed defense economics head, developed the first jet fighter plane in 1940, the Me 262. Later it was assembled in the Dora-Mittelbau concentration camp. After the war Messerschmitt designed aircraft for the Federal German Armed Forces. His company was merged into the Messerschmitt-Bölkow-Blohm firm. He died in 1978.

HENRIETTE VON SCHIRACH

Daughter of Heinrich Hoffmann and wife of Baldur von Schirach. Born 1913 in Munich, she lived with her husband in Berlin and, from 1940, in Vienna. After the war she sought work in the film industry. Henriette von Schirach died in 1992.

CARL SEVERING

Social Democrat politician and Prussian minister of the interior. Born 1875 in Herford, from 1893 member of the Social Democratic Party (SPD). From 1907 to 1911 Severing was a deputy in the Reichstag. In 1920 Severing became Prussian minister of the interior for the first time, in 1928 he was promoted to Reich minister of the interior, and in 1930 he took over the Prussian Ministry of the Interior again. In 1932, after Franz von Papen's "Prussian coup," Severing lost his position, and in 1933 he was briefly imprisoned, and retired from politics. Later he was accused of having put up too little resistance to the threat of the National Socialists. After the war Severing was an SPD deputy in the North Rhine–Westphalian Landtag. He died in Bielefeld in 1952.

MARIE-CLAUDE VAILLANT-COUTURIER

Auschwitz survivor and French parliamentary deputy. Born 1912 in Paris, she worked as a photojournalist and joined the French Résistance to the German occupation. Vaillant-Couturier was arrested in February 1942, and in January 1943 she was sent to Auschwitz. After the war she was a communist deputy in the National Constituent Assembly. Vaillant-Couturier died in 1996.

ERNST VON WEIZSÄCKER

State secretary in the Foreign Office and German ambassador to the Holy See. Born in Stuttgart in 1882, Weizsäcker entered the service of the Foreign Office in 1920. In March of that year he became state secretary in the Foreign Ministry, and joined the National Socialist Party a month later. From June 1943 Weizsäcker was German ambassador at the Vatican in Rome. In the Wilhelmstrasse Trial, Weizsäcker was sentenced to seven years in prison for approving bureaucratic measures of aid for the deportation of Jews. In October 1950, after serving just over a year of his sentence, he was released early. Weizsäcker died in Lindau in 1951. His son, Richard von Weizsäcker, who worked on his legal defense team at Nuremberg, went on to become the first president of reunified Germany in 1990.

BIBLIOGRAPHY

Bancroft, Mary. *Autobiography of a Spy.* William Morrow & Co., New York, 1983.

Bedürftig, Friedemann. *Drittes Reich und Zweiter Weltkrieg.* Das Lexikon, Piper Verlag, Munich, 2002.

Benz, Wolfgang, Hermann Graml, and Hermann Weiss. *Enzyklopädie des Nationalsozialismus.* Deutscher Taschenbuch Verlag, Munich, 1997.

Buchheim, Hans, Martin Broszat, Hans-Adolf Jacobsen, and Helmut Krausnick. *Anatomie Des SS-Staates.* Deutscher Taschenbuch Verlag, Munich, 1967. Seventh edition, May 1999.

D'Addario, Ray, and Klaus Kastner. *Der Nürnberger Prozess—Das Verfahren gegen die Hauptkriegsverbrecher 1945–1946.* Verlag A. Hoffmann, Nuremberg, 1994.

Dastrup, Boyd L. *Crusade in Nuremberg—Military Occupation 1945–1949.* Greenwood Press, Westport, Connecticut, 1985.

Echtenkamp, Jörg. *Nach dem Krieg—Alltagsnot, Neuorientierung und die Last der Vergangenheit 1945–1949.* Pendo Verlag, Zürich, 2003.

Gaskin, Hillary. *Eyewitness at Nuremberg.* Arms and Armour Press, London, 1990.

Gilbert, Gustave M. *Nuremberg Diary.* Farrar, Straus & Co., New York, 1947.

Gisevius, Hans Bernd. *To the Bitter End.* Translated by Richard and Clara Winston. Houghton Mifflin Co., Boston, 1947.

———. *Wo ist Nebe? Erinnerungen an Hitlers Reichskriminaldirektor.* Droemersche Verlagsanstalt, Zürich, 1966.

Glaubauf, Karl, and Stefanie Lahousen. *Generalmajor Erwin Lahousen Edler von Vivremont—Ein Linzer Abwehroffcier im militärischen Widerstand*. Lit. Verlag, Münster, 2004.

Haase, Günther. *Die Kunstsammlung des Marschalls Hermann Göring*. Quintessenz Verlag GmbH, Berlin, 2000.

Haensel, Carl. *Der Nürnberger Prozess—Tagebuch eines Verteidigers*. Möwig Taschenbuch Verlag, Munich/Rastatt, 1983. First edition, Claassen Verlag, Hamburg, 1950.

Haffner, Sebastian. *Germany: Jekyll & Hyde*. Libris, London, 2005.

Heigl, Peter. *Nürnberger Prozesse*. Verlag Hans Carl, Nuremberg, 2001.

Herz, Rudolf. *Hoffmann & Hitler—Fotographie als Medium des Führer-Mythos*. Verlag Klinkhardt & Biermann, Munich, 1994.

Heydecker, Joe J., and Johannes Leeb. *The Nuremberg Trial*. Translated by R. A. Downie. World Publishing, Cleveland, 1962.

Höhne, Heinz. *Der Orden unter dem Totenkopf—Die Geschichte der SS*. Bertelsmann Verlag, Munich, 1987.

Höss, Rudolf. *Kommandant in Auschwitz, Autobiografische Aufzeichnungen des Rudolf Höss*. Edited by Martin Broszat. Deutscher Taschenbuch Verlag, Munich, 1998.

Hunecke, Douglas K. *In Deutschland unerwünscht—Hermann Gräbe, Biografie eines Judenretter*. Klampen Verlag, Lüneburg, 2002.

Internationaler Militärgerichtshof Nürnberg. *Der Nürnberger Prozess gegen die Hauptkriegsverbrecher vom 14. November 1945-1. Oktober 1946*. Reichenbach Verlag, Nuremberg, 1947.

Jäckel, Eberhard, Peter Longerich, and Julius H. Schoeps. *Enzyklopädie des Holocaust*. Piper Verlag, Munich, 2002.

Junge, Traudl. *Until the Final Hour: Hitler's Last Secretary*. Edited by Melissa Müller. Translated by Anthea Bell. Weidenfeld & Nicolson, London, 2003.

Kálnoky, Ingeborg, and Ilona Herisko. *The Guest House*. Bobbs-Merrill Co., Inc., New York, 1975.

Kempner, Robert M. W. *Anklager einer Epoche, Lebenerinnerungen*. In collaboration with Jörg Friedrich. Ullstein Verlag, Frankfurt/Main, Berlin, 1986.

———. *Das Dritte Reich im Kreuzverhör*. Athenäum Verlag, Königstein, 1969.

Kershaw, Ian. *Hitler, 1889–1936: Hubris*. Allen Lane, The Penguin Press, London, 1998.

———. *Hitler, 1936–1945: Nemesis*. Allen Lane, The Penguin Press, London, 2000.

Knopp, Guido. *Hitlers Helfer*. C. Bertelsmann Verlag, Munich, 1996.

Kogon, Eugen. *The Theory and Practice of Hell*. Translated by Heinz Norden. Farrar, Straus & Giroux, New York, 1966.

Lester, Jane. *An American College Girl in Hitler's Germany*. The Edwin Mellen Press, Lewiston, New York, 1999.

Lippe, Viktor von der. *Nürnberger Tagebuchnotizen—November 1945 bis Oktober 1946*. Verlag Fritz Knapp, Frankfurt/Main, 1951.

Lohalm, Uwe, and Michael Wildt, editors, for the Forschungsstelle für Zeitgeschichte, Hamburg. *Der Dienstkalender Heinrich Himmlers 1941/42*. Hans Christians Verlag, Hamburg, 1999.

Metcalfe, Philip. *1933*. The Permanent Press, New York, 1988.

Mühlen, Bengt von der. *Der Todeskampf der Reichshauptstadt*. Chronos-Film GmbH, Berlin-Kleinmachnow, 1994.

OMGUS (Office of Military Government for Germany, United States), U.S. Group Control Council—Finance Division. *Ermittlungen gegen die I.G. Farbenindustrie AG*. September 1945. Special volume, Die Andere Bibliothek, edited by Hans Magnus Enzensberger. Greno Verlag, Nördlingen, 1986.

Padover, Saul K. *Lügendetektor—Vernehmungen im besiegten Deutschland 1944/45*. Die Andere Bibliothek, Eichborn Verlag, Frankfurt, 1999.

Persico, Joseph E. *Nuremberg—Infamy on Trial*. Penguin Books, New York, 1994.

Radlmaier, Steffen. *Die Nürnberger Lernprozess—Von Kriegsverbrechern und Starreportern*. Die Andere Bibliothek, Eichborn Verlag, Frankfurt, 2001.

Shirer, William L. *Berlin Diary: Journal of a Foreign Correspondent*. Johns Hopkins University Press, Baltimore, 1941.

———. *The Rise and Fall of the Third Reich: A History of Nazi Germany*. Simon & Schuster, New York, 1960.

Sigmund, Anna Maria. *Die Frauen der Nazis*. Ueberreuter Verlag, Vienna, 1998.

Sonnenfeldt, Richard W. *Witness to Nuremberg*. Arcade Publishing, New York, 2006.

Taylor, Telford. *An Anatomy of the Nuremberg Trials: A Personal Memoir*. Knopf, New York, 1992.

Ueberschär, Gerd R. *NS-Verbrechen und der militärische Widerstand gegen Hitler*. Primus Verlag, Darmstadt, 2000.

Vaccaro, Tony. *Entering Germany 1944–1949*. Taschen Verlag, Cologne, 2001.

Völklein, Ulrich. *Die Weizsäckers. Macht und Moral—Portät einer deutschen Familie*. Droemer Verlag, Munich, 2004.

Weiss, Hermann. *Biographisches Lexikon zum Dritten Reich*. S. Fischer Verlag, Frankfurt, 1998.

West, Rebecca. "Greenhouse with Cyclamens." In *A Train of Powder*. Macmillan, London, 1955. Published originally in 1946 in *The New Yorker*.

PICTURE CREDITS

INDEX

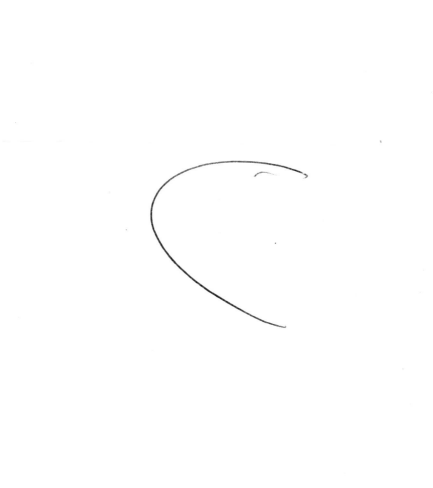